HOW TO TAKE
MONSTER BUCKS

Secrets To Finding Trophy Deer

by John E. Phillips

ISBN 0-936513-46-2

Library of Congress 94-72944

Published by:

LARSEN'S OUTDOOR PUBLISHING
2640 Elizabeth Place
Lakeland, FL 33813

PRINTED IN THE UNITED STATES OF AMERICA

1 2 3 4 5 6 7 8 9 10

DEDICATION

The future of the world depends on the character, patience, dedication, understanding and more importantly the work ethic of our young people. Because I believe in the youth of this country, I employ interns from major universities in my area to work with me.

But Carmine Berry is different. As a senior in high school, she came to work for me after school and on Saturdays to earn spending money. After choosing journalism as her major, she enrolled in Samford University's journalism department and continued to work with me to defray school expenses. With the same dedication, professionalism and hard work she has shown since high school, she has labored shoulder to shoulder with us to complete this book.

For these and many more reasons this work is dedicated to Carmine Berry. Thanks, pal!

ACKNOWLEDGMENTS

Many have worked long and hard to help bring materials, photography, knowledge and experience into the pages of this book. Without these people, years may have overtaken enthusiasm, and the book may have been no more than a good idea lying on a shelf. The success of any book is directly related to the people involved, not only in its writing, photography and graphics but in its overall production. To these people I want to say thank you: Denise Phillips, Marjolyn McLellan, Ellery Cook, Julie Bowlin, Carol Price, Lisa Wells, Larry and Lilliam Larsen, Jim Tostrud and Kelly Breland.

CONTENTS

Dedication 3
Acknowledgments 3
Preface 7
About the Author 9
About the Artist 10

1 THE CHALLENGE OF HUNTING
  TROPHY BUCKS 11

2 WHERE HAVE YOUR TROPHY BUCKS GONE? 19

3 SELECT THE BEST STAND SITE
  FOR MONSTER-SIZED BUCKS 29

4 CACKLE UP A BIG BUCK 39

5 SHOOT TROPHY BUCKS ON THE RUN 47

6 USE MAN-DRIVES FOR
  MONSTER-SIZED BUCKS 59

7 DOUBLE CALL TO BAG BIG BUCKS 69

8 TRACK TROPHY BUCKS IN THE SNOW 77

9 HUNT CATTLE COUNTRY FOR
  MONSTER-SIZED BUCKS 89

10 USE YOUR TABLE-TOP TO BAG BIG BUCKS 99

11 ROAD HUNT TO TAKE TROPHY BUCKS 107

12 HUNT WETLANDS FOR BIG BUCKS 115

13 FIND MONSTER BUCKS IN CROPLANDS 125

14 HUNT LATE-SEASON PRESSURED BIG BUCKS ... 135

15 BEWARE OF HUMAN ODOR
   WHEN HUNTING BIG BUCKS 145

   Index 151
   Resource Directory 153

PREFACE

The trophy buck usually is at least 3-years old or older. Generally a monster buck will be five years old or older. These big bucks:

* Have survived many hunter encounters.
* Know what the hunter will do before he does.
* Have lived long enough to recognize danger signs.
* Have stored up a wealth of information about hunters that allows them to survive.
* Make fewer mistakes than the younger bucks that haven't lived as long or dodged hunters as often.
* Will feed and move primarily at night in open woodlots.
* Move during daylight in thick cover most hunters can't penetrate.
* Won't work their scrape lines during daylight as do younger bucks.
* Rarely use regular deer trails, even to go to food sources.
* Hole up in areas where no one thinks a big buck will be.

Trophy-class bucks are extremely sensitive to hunter pressure. If a majestic buck sees or smells you, it's a good bet he won't return to that site that year. Although the trophy buck, like any other buck, is a creature of habit, he is much quicker than a younger deer to change his habits or haunts when he spots you or winds you.

Strong evidence indicates that more of the bigger, older bucks with heavy antlers die from natural causes or from combat than are taken by hunters. Remember, an older buck is the smartest, most elusive deer in the woods. He's escaped from every hunter who has come after him.

The older a buck becomes, the more likely he is to die of old age. The only exception is when he crosses into another trophy buck's territory or another big buck moves into his territory. When two bucks die with their antlers locked, they are usually older bucks no one has seen there before. When you find the skull of a buck with a large, heavy rack, often you can assume that the buck died after combat with another trophy buck.

You can bag monster-sized bucks by following the ideas in this book.

ABOUT THE AUTHOR

For more than three decades, John E. Phillips has hunted the white-tailed deer. Phillips explains that, ''I even chose to attend Livingston University in deer-rich Southwest Alabama so I could deer hunt at least four days a week from mid-October until the last day of January all during my college years until I graduated.''

Phillips also has been a student of deer and deer hunting as a parttime taxidermist and an active outdoor writer and photographer for more than 20 years for both newspapers and magazines. Phillips, the author of 18-other outdoor books including: ''The Masters' Secrets of Turkey Hunting,'' ''Outdoor Life's Complete Turkey Hunting,'' ''Turkey Tactics,'' ''Turkey Hunter's Bible,'' ''The Masters' Secrets of Deer Hunting,'' ''The Science of Deer Hunting,'' ''Deer and Fixings,'' The Masters' Secrets of Bowhunting Deer,'' ''Jim Crumley's Bowhunting Secrets,'' ''Alabama Outdoors Cookbook,'' ''How to Make More Profits in Taxidermy,'' ''Catch MoreCrappie,'' ''The Masters' Secrets of Crappie Fishing,'' ''Bass Fishing with the Skeeter Pros,'' ''Fish and Fixings,'' ''The Masters' Secrets of Catfishing,'' ''Bass Fishing Central Alabama'' and ''Black-Powder Hunting Secrets,'' has had more than 1,000 articles published on hunting deer. An active member of Outdoor Writers Association of America, Southeastern Outdoors Press Association, Alabama Press Association and Outdoors Photographic League, Phillips has won numerous awards for excellence in writing magazine and newspaper articles and outdoor books.

According to Phillips, ''I've been fortunate enough to hunt with some of the greatest deer hunters of our day, which has made me have an insatiable passion for the sport.''

Phillips has taken deer with bow and arrow, blackpowder rifles, shotguns and conventional rifles. He has hunted the mountains, plains, swamps, forests and croplands of the U.S. Phillips has learned the art of deer hunting from some of the best hunters in the nation and has brought this knowledge to you in ''How to Take Monster Bucks.''

ABOUT THE ARTIST

Thirty-two year old Jim Tostrud of Kenosha, Wisconsin, the artist whose work is featured on the cover and also the inside of "HOW TO TAKE MONSTER BUCKS," grew up in Wisconsin very interested in wildlife and the outdoors.

According to Tostrud, "I grew up hunting and fishing and developed a special love for God's wild creatures. One of the reasons I chose to be a wildlife artist was because I felt I could promote the importance of conservation and management of our wildlife through my artwork.--"However, the main reason of my work is to convey the beauty and wonder of nature to the people who view my art. I am very grateful to the Lord for the subjects I portray and the ability to bring them back to life on canvas."

A graduate of Viterbo Fine Arts College in LaCrosse, Wisconsin, Tostrud's work shows the intense love he has for the animals he portrays. He pays close attention to every detail of his subject and the natural setting in which it is found. As Tostrud explained, "I want all my pieces to be aesthetically pleasing and yet trigger a reaction from the viewer."

Honored by Whitetails Unlimited as the organization's Artist of the Year in 1993-94, Tostrud also is the staff artist for "Wisconsin Woods

and Waters Magazine" and a member of the Wellington Pro Staff and is active in many non-profit conservation organizations such as Pheasants Forever and Ducks Unlimited.

Contact Jim Tostrud at 1787 15th Avenue, Kenosha, WI 53140, (414) 657-7099, about his original oils, acrylics, pencil and pen and ink drawings as well as his limited editions and prints.

CHAPTER 1

THE CHALLENGE OF HUNTING TROPHY BUCKS

Deer hunting's hand of fate deals various cards to different sportsmen. Occasionally, fate will deal an ace that results in some lucky hunter's bagging a trophy deer. But to consistently take trophies -- the big, wide-racked, heavy-antlered bucks -- requires a special breed of men who have matured as hunters and who will pay an exciting price. The trophy deer hunter is a breed apart.

Every deer hunter has one goal when he first begins hunting -- to take a buck -- any buck. After the rite of passage of bagging a buck, the sportsman finds himself initiated into the deer-hunting fraternity. In the next phase hunters pass through, they want to take as many bucks as legally possible, which may mean traveling to different states, hunting on hunting preserves and spending thousands of dollars to prove to themselves that not only can they bag bucks but that they can take bucks regularly.

Then the woodman's hunting generally follows one of two routes. If he has the money and the time, he will try to collect as many trophy-sized bucks as he can by traveling across the country and paying high fees to kill big bucks that have lived protected on private lands. The outdoorsman who takes the other route will attempt to learn all he can about the lands he hunts, search for trophy deer on them and try to bag them.

These two philosophies cross again when the deer hunter finally reaches maturity and becomes a true trophy-buck hunter. He no longer has to prove that he can kill a deer, many deer or a trophy deer. Now his hunt emphasizes taking the best trophy buck, the biggest deer in the woods, the animal no one else seems capable of bagging, that one giant stag other hunters believe lives in a woodlot that they may have spotted for only fleeting moments.

To deserve the name trophy buck hunter, a sportsman must become a master woodsman with skills, patience and perception that outdistances the other hunters who go into the woods in hopes of bagging a whitetail. The trophy deer hunter hunts like a chess master plays. He studies his opponent with as much diligence as he studies the game itself. To win and claim the prize, the trophy deer hunter plays well and outthinks and out-reasons the competition.

The Trophy Buck: A Clear Definition

But before defining a trophy-whitetail hunter, we must first learn the characteristics of a trophy deer and then determine an area where we can locate this trophy animal before we come up with the tactics to take him. Usually a trophy deer has lived more than three years because he has had time to put on body weight and grow large antlers. The gene pool in his region historically must have produced trophy deer. Often other hunters may see this buck that has managed to elude all who have hunted him.

To begin the search for a trophy buck, generally a seasoned woodsman will talk to other hunters and consult with the wildlife biologists in his state or in the state he plans to hunt. Because of soil type, history of the region, availability of land and food and hunting pressure, most biologists accurately can predict where in a state trophy bucks should occur.

The soil type, if it has enough nutrition and minerals in it, can produce the food to yield heavy body weights and large antler development. A range not overpopulated with deer should have enough food available for the trophy buck to reach his maximum size in three to five years. A sportsman can increase his chances of taking a big buck by hunting regions of less extensive hunting pressure and low numbers of deer. If the history of the area reveals that this particular place

You can take trophy bucks like this one if you're willing to let smaller bucks pass.

traditionally has produced trophy bucks, then the gene pool of the herd can yield another trophy for the woodsman willing to go after the animal.

The Trophy Deer Hunter: A Description

Now that we have defined the animal the trophy buck hunter plans to hunt, let's look at what the sportsman must do to consistently bag this type of deer. The most difficult test most trophy hunters must pass involves their letting nice bucks walk when searching for a trophy. The trophy hunter's dedication to hunting a trophy means the outdoorsman must back his finger off the trigger when a nice 6- or 8-point buck walks to within easy killing distance. He realizes the trophy buck may stand behind or in close proximity to these other whitetails. The trophy hunter must deny himself the right to take good bucks to bag that one trophy deer for which he searches.

Also the trophy hunter must have the patience of Job. He may have to sit in a tree stand or a ground blind for 10 to 12 consecutive days without ever seeing a deer in hopes that one trophy buck will come his way. He must endure ridicule and persecution from his friends, most of whom will take bucks each season before he does and then will kid him about his not having bagged his buck as the end of the season nears.

The trophy hunter must let the deer he hunts become an obsession to learn to think like the deer he stalks. The woodsman must abandon the usual hunting practices of the area he hunts, because he knows that only by hunting this trophy buck at various times with different methods and often in a different place will he have the chance of succeeding when others have failed to take the trophy buck.

The trophy buck hunter finds his sport solitary. Few others understand the rules of his game. I admire these men, these ultimate deer hunters who are a breed apart.

The Trophy-Buck Researcher

A good trophy deer hunter is very much like Sherlock Holmes, because he constantly digs for information, searches for clues, tries to put together formulas, attempts to reason like his quarry and goes through all the mental gymnastics a good detective must to crack a case. Often a trophy-buck hunter will begin his hunt for a true trophy deer in the wee hours of the night. At this time, the biggest deer will leave their sanctuaries and move out into fields and pastures to feed. In the states that permit hunters to shine lights after dark over fields, the hunter quickly can see if a trophy buck lives in the area he plans to hunt. Then his investigation begins.

The woodsman will attempt to discover where the big buck leaves the field and enters the woods by following his tracks. Many times the trophy buck uses a trail to go back and forth to and from the field. But the field provides only a beginning place for the trophy-buck researcher. From that point on, he must use all the knowledge he can acquire about that particular deer to set up an ambush point.

Like many other outdoorsmen, I believe some smart bucks actually die of old age in heavily hunted areas. These bucks only move and feed after dark and will hole up in thick cover all day long. When hunting season starts, these deer become completely nocturnal. Then the hunter

Ronnie Strickland, of West Point, Mississippi, took this gorilla-sized buck by hunting in a clearcut in pouring rain when few would have hunted.

has no chance of bagging them. The sportsman must research to see if he can take a stand anywhere in the woods to catch that buck moving during daylight hours.

However, a hunter may harvest a nocturnal buck during the rut, because the trophy buck is usually the biggest, oldest and smartest deer in the herd. By the right of dominance, he has the responsibility of breeding the does. When the rut takes place, the trophy buck must leave cover to breed the does. The hunter in search of a trophy in the rut must begin his research along well-worn trails where he finds scrapes and in areas where he most likely will see does, which means bucks naturally will appear at these sites during the breeding season.

A trophy buck taker I knew had hunted a granddaddy buck for a long time. Everything he had tried had failed. Finally during the rut, he reasoned that the bucks had to hang around the does, to breed the females when they came in estrus. Therefore, he decided that if he found and followed the does, sooner or later a buck had to appear.

With this in mind, he donned his camo, painted his tennis shoes green, bought a good pair of binoculars and went into the woods to hunt. After finding a group of eight does feeding through a hardwood bottom, he dedicated himself to staying with those deer until he either spooked them or they led him to a buck.

Later he told me, "My eyes nearly crossed from watching those does. But finally as the deer passed through the bottom and headed into an area where a tornado had blown down some trees, I looked into the top of one of those downed trees with my binoculars. I spotted the ivory-colored antlers of a trophy-sized buck. I believe the buck knew where the does would feed. I think he waited there for them to show up to put himself in the right place at the best time to breed a doe.

"I watched that antler tip for awhile. As the does fed from the tree, the buck stood up, stretched himself and started looking in the direction the does had gone, as if to follow them. I took him. Since that time I have practiced following does to get to trophy bucks. Although I may trail deer for the better part of a day and never see a buck, every now and then, those does will lead me to the big buck I'm hunting."

The Clear-Cut Specialist

One of the most dedicated trophy hunters I have known I have dubbed the Clear-Cut Specialist. He bags big bucks from clearcuts that have grown up in brush, briars and bushes. Although deer love these kinds of areas, hunters hate them. Big bucks inhabit these regions because the spots provide everything they need -- food, shelter, often water and especially sanctuary. A man who consistently takes trophy deer from a clearcut must be a step above the average deer hunter.

"I have several tactics I use to hunt clear-cut bucks," a veteran brush hunter told me. "Depending on the clearcut, I apply the appropriate method. For instance the Western hunter must utilize a spotting scope. But in the East, most outdoorsmen look at you funny if you use a spotting scope anywhere except on the rifle range.

"However, I've discovered if I can find a mountain or a hill above a clearcut, I can set up a spotting scope on the ridge and spend hours carefully looking down into the clearcut to locate deer. Although the process may take me three or four hours to study a clearcut of 40 to 80 acres thoroughly, many times I can spot an ear tip, the inside of a deer's ear or the black circle of his eye from several hundred yards away.

A dream buck like this can be yours if you pay the price and hunt hard -- (Drawing by Jim Tostrud).

"Once I observe the deer, I can determine the best way of hunting him. I can hunt clearcuts in the middle of the day when the deer generally don't move but instead bed down, in the early morning hours when the deer come back from feeding or in the late afternoon when the big bucks prepare to leave the thicket to begin their nightly feedings.

"If no ridge, hill or other vantage point lies near the clearcut, then I have a problem. Often I will utilize a small hatchet to cut three 30- to 40-yard shooting lanes that spoke out from a central position. Then I can sit inside the dense cover and see any deer that cross any of the lanes. But I never cut an entrance lane into the clearcut. I don't want any other hunter to get into that thick cover and discover an ambush spot."

The Public Land Hunter

This trophy hunter goes into some of the most intensely hunted areas in his state -- wildlife management areas. He realizes that when the hunters come into the woods the older, bigger, smarter trophy bucks head for thick cover. To take those deer, he goes into that cover, climbs a tree well before daylight and remains in that tree until after dark.

"At some time during the day I generally begin to see deer," the public-land specialist explained. "Most of the deer movement occurs at daylight when the hunters move into the woods to go to lunch and just before dark when the hunters go home from the woods.

"Big bucks will not stay in areas of high hunting pressure but must move to heavy cover. To bag a trophy deer, I find the heaviest cover I can on public-hunting regions and let the other sportsmen force the deer to come to me. Sooner or later during the day, I generally will have the opportunity for a shot. However, most of the time I won't shoot, when the bucks I see sport spikes, 4 points or 6 points. I want to protect these seed bucks in those thick places so they will become trophy deer.

"When I spot one of the smaller deer coming through the thicket, I just grin and say to myself, 'You're doing well, young friend. Keep up the good work. In a few years you'll be a trophy. In a few years, maybe our paths will cross again.'"

No shortcuts exist for taking trophy bucks on public lands. The trophy buck taker must get into the thick places, remain there all day long and maintain a high level of concentration. He only may get one glimpse of that buck of a lifetime.

A Trophy Hunter's Nightmare

One of the best trophy hunters I know told me of a terrible experience that happened to him last season.

"I had seen a huge buck twice in a thicket where I hunted but never could get a shot at him. I had found his shed antlers, seen his scrapes, and followed his tracks. I assumed in a matter of time I would catch up with him -- hopefully his last season. Finally I located my trophy in a thicket about 150 yards from my property line. Someone had killed him but not recovered him. The big buck already had decomposed, and squirrels had begun to gnaw on his massive antlers. I almost became sick to my stomach. This prize animal, a deer I stalked for three years and had come to know and understand, had been wasted. I lost the opportunity to take him and preserve his rack forever, and no longer would I have the chance to hunt him and pit my wits against his."

Trophy hunters, a rare breed themselves, hunt these unique deer by utilizing unusual tactics. They don't take many deer. Some seasons they may not bag any bucks. But when a trophy hunter comes home with the trunk of his car cracked, a trophy buck lies in the back.

CHAPTER 2

WHERE HAVE YOUR TROPHY BUCKS GONE?

For most of us, those big buck mounts on display at deer shows and in trophy rooms are like fleeting daydreams. They seem as far removed from reality as winning the lottery.

But are huge bucks truly rare across North America? I'm not talking about proven trophy-producing ranches, untapped river-bottoms or remote wilderness forests. I mean the big bucks in your home state or my home state of Alabama. Are big bucks just not there? If they are, why are these magnificent animals seldom seen or shot?

In some areas, trophy bucks exist in minuscule numbers. But from what I've seen, every state produces several big bucks each year. Some hunters and researchers believe many of the greatest trophy bucks that ever have lived -- or are living today -- have died or will die of old age, not from a hunter's bullet or broadhead.

Although such bucks probably have had many near-death encounters, their senses, instinct, adaptability and resourcefulness have enabled them to dodge danger successfully. Sometimes these bucks appear to be too tough to be killed.

Orrin J. Rongstad - Research in Wisconsin

Orrin J. Rongstad, professor emeritus in wildlife ecology at the University of Wisconsin-Madison, is convinced many old bucks die of natural causes each year throughout the United States. Rongstad did not always hold that opinion. In fact, as recently as the mid-1980s, Rongstad scoffed when Wisconsin biologists speculated that many bucks died of old age in the state's Northern Forest. There was little physical evidence or eyewitness testimony to support the claim.

"I used to chuckle when they said we had all these old bucks dying up north in our state," Rongstad said. "I didn't believe it. Now I do. Those older bucks just aren't being killed by hunters."

What made Rongstad change his mind? The answer is found in his ongoing research using radio telemetry. The research started in 1986 when Rongstad and his group of graduate students began trapping and radio-tagging deer in the forests of northwestern Wisconsin. The number of tagged deer had grown to 266 by 1993.

Originally, the tagging program was designed to determine the effects of artificial feeding on deer, to learn their movement patterns and to assess their ability to survive. But for the past three to four years, Rongstad also has been watching for some clues about the long-term survival of deer tagged early in the study.

"Our research shows many older bucks are not being harvested," Rongstad explained. "The percentage of radio-tagged bucks killed by hunters is so low that there has to be a bunch of them up there.

"We found one buck last year that was at least 9.5 years old that had died from natural causes. He had a severe infection on top of his head around the base of his antlers, which could have been caused from a buck fight or some other injury. But in general, he wasn't showing his age. His teeth weren't worn badly, and his body was in good shape."

But Rongstad is quick to say he does not know the actual causes of death for older bucks, mainly because their bodies are seldom found. (In many cases, the transmitters stop functioning, or the deer vanish from where they have been trapped, making tracking them impossible).

Rongstad reported 40 bucks from the research's early years still unaccounted for as he commented, "Some of those bucks were 3.5 years old in 1986. If they were taken by hunters, I think most hunters would have reported the incidents and turned in the tags or collars. But we haven't heard anything about those bucks since we tagged them. If they are still alive, they will be 9 or 10 years old. I believe many of them have died from old age by now."

The sad but true fact is that many trophy bucks die of old age (Drawing by Jim Tostrud).

If old bucks are dying of natural causes, why don't we find them or their skeletons? Rongstad offers two possibilities:

"If these bucks eluded hunters for many years by remaining in heavy cover, then we can reason that when they're hurt or injured, they'll return to their sanctuaries to die," Rongstad said. "Since hunters never has discovered that sanctuary when the buck is alive, we can assume they won't find him after he dies.

"Another possibility is that predators and scavengers such as dogs, bobcats, raccoons, foxes and coyotes feed on the carcasses and chew and scatter the bones. Also rodents like rats, squirrels and porcupines probably eat the bones and antlers."

If Rongstad is right about older bucks dying of natural causes, one possible effect is that harvest data collected by hunters and state wildlife agencies may not provide a totally accurate picture of a herd's age structure. Biologists usually assume that when the percentage of older animals in the hunters' harvest is low, it represents a low number of older animals in the herd.

James Kroll & Ben Koerth - Deer Biologists

Two researchers who question that assumption are Professor James C. Kroll and Ben Koerth, a research associate, at the College of Forestry at Stephen F. Austin State University in Nacogdoches, Texas. Kroll and Koerth are in the second year of a five-year study that compares the university's age-structure data on white-tailed does with data compiled separately by hunting clubs and the Texas Parks and Wildlife Department.

Kroll and Koerth found no significant difference between data collected by hunters and data collected by the department. That means these data provide an accurate picture of the age structure of harvested deer. However, they believe harvest data do not necessarily reflect the actual age structure of the herd.

"We are seeing some definite hunter bias in harvest data," Kroll said. "Apparently, does in the mature prime-age classes (4 to 5 years of age) are significantly under-represented in the hunters' harvest; and we continue to see significantly fewer two-year-olds in our own samples than reported by hunters and the department."

Koerth believes the university's data is most accurate because the does in this sample are shot randomly at night under a special research permit.

"That's why we see a lot more older deer in our sample than what hunters see in theirs," Koerth reported.

The same trends surface with bucks. Kroll says these differences are caused by a tendency for hunters to kill less experienced animals.

"The older bucks out there aren't going to show up as much in the hunters' harvests," Koerth mentioned. "The older deer aren't the first ones to walk out in broad daylight and get shot. That means the age structure of bucks in the herd is different from the bucks that are harvested. More older bucks are out there than what is represented in the harvest."

Bob Zaiglin - Texas Wildlife Scientist

Researcher Bob Zaiglin, of Uvalde, Texas, manages several southern Texas ranches for quality bucks. He has studied older bucks more than 20 years, and has drawn some interesting conclusions.

Older age-class bucks move primarily at night and are rarely seen in daylight hours.

"Various factors enable some bucks to live to old ages," Zaiglin said. "Reaching hard and fast conclusions is extremely difficult. In general, deer in the North and Northeast experience more hunting pressure than deer in parts of the South and, particularly the Southwest, where hunter access is much more limited. By limiting hunting pressure, more bucks can survive to older ages.

"But no matter where you hunt, certain individual deer have an inherent ability to dodge hunters. I don't know whether the deer's ability to escape hunters is learned from the past, or whether certain bucks are born with an elusiveness that allows them to survive.

"Some bucks are naturally more nocturnal than others, but others become nocturnal in response to hunting pressure. If a buck tends to be nocturnal and he also has an inherent ability to dodge hunters, he will be almost impossible to bag. He'll likely die from old age."

As Zaiglin said, though, some parts of the country produce more older bucks than others, primarily because of differences in hunting pressure.

"In areas with high hunting pressure, the largest percentage of bucks harvested are 1.5-year-old animals," he noted.

Zaiglin explains that three primary factors enable quality bucks to avoid a hunter's bullet or arrow until natural causes kill them: hunting pressure, survival instincts and a tendency to be more nocturnal than other bucks.

Zaiglin and Rongstad agree that the more hunter-encounters a buck survives, the sharper his survival instincts become. In other words, the chances that the buck will be killed by hunters decrease with his age.

Many hunting groups on private lands and leased properties are setting strict standards for bucks that hunters can shoot. Some clubs require hunters to hold their fire unless the buck carries 8 or more points or has a main-beam span of at least 16 inches. By not shooting the younger bucks, more bucks reach older ages. This practice can increase the hunters' opportunities for shooting a quality buck, while improving the herd's age structure and buck-to-doe ratio.

However, one factor the hunters too often forget is that these same older bucks become more elusive each hunting season. Therefore, if hunters restrict the kill of younger bucks to improve the herd's quality, they must accept that some of those bucks will evade them forever.

"Most hunters learn to pattern deer so they can try to predict where the animals will show up," Zaiglin said. "They often forget the deer also pattern the hunters. Through the years, some animals learn which places and at what time of the year they encounter hunters. When that time of year comes, they'll avoid those areas. These 'Rambo' bucks may die of old age."

Steve Demarais - Texas Tech Researcher

In one of Zaiglin's studies, he and Texas Tech professor Steve Demarais radio-collared 25 bucks on a 100,000-acre ranch and studied them between 1986 and 1989. At the time of the tagging, the bucks ranged from 3.5- to 7.5-years old, with an average age of 4.5 years. During the four years of the study, 10 of the bucks died. The dead bucks ranged in age from 3.5 to 8.5 years, with an average of 6.6 years. One of the 10 that died was mortally wounded during a fight with another mature buck.

24

If this buck had not been harvested, he might have died of natural causes.

Demarais -- who works in Texas Tech's Department of Range and Wildlife Management in Lubbock -- said none of the 10 bucks that died was killed by hunters, mainly because hunting on the property is tightly restricted. Instead, most of the deaths were likely caused by post-rut stresses, he said. In herds where competition is keen between mature bucks for breeding privileges, they can run themselves ragged during the rut. Afterward, until they recuperate, they're often susceptible to disease and coyote predation.

Harry Jacobson - Mississippi Wildlife Biologist

Professor Harry Jacobson of the Department of Wildlife and Fisheries at Mississippi State University has conducted a buck mortality study the past three years. He plans to continue it through 1997. In addition, he has conducted radio telemetry studies on deer the past 17 years. Although Jacobson's current mortality study is still in the preliminary stages, he has begun to draw some conclusions about mortality in older bucks.

"In our study, we have seen very little mortality that's not hunter- or poacher-related," Jacobson said. "The small amount of natural mortality we've found has been relatively insignificant. We've only had two or three animals so far that have died naturally out of 156 collared deer. Also, our sample size was relatively low on older bucks, with probably only 20 animals 4 years or older in it.

"The deer we've collared receive some protection because we've asked hunters not to shoot them. However, we still see substantial mortality caused by hunters. Out of the 156 bucks we've fitted with transmitters, we've had 80 of them shot by poachers or hunters. Even though we ask hunters not to shoot these deer, some of them seem to make this mistake when they see a bigger buck."

Still, Jacobson reports that most hunters in the study area honor the researchers' requests not to shoot collared bucks. "One club kicked out a member last year after he shot a collared buck. They didn't throw him out because he killed the deer. They did it because he lied about how he shot it, and he tried to hide the collar."

Jacobson's research verifies that the amount of hunting pressure is directly related to the number of older bucks on the property.

"Intense hunting pressure prevents most bucks from reaching the older-age classes," Jacobson said.

He agrees with Rongstad and Zaiglin that older bucks adapt quickly to hunting pressure.

"An individual buck may become totally nocturnal," he observed. "Also, some older animals find a sanctuary to dodge hunters during the hunting season and are never seen. Unless the hunter accidentally bumps into one of these bucks, no one will take these deer. The one exception is the rut. Bucks become more vulnerable at that time."

Jacobson hopes some of the tagged deer still will be alive when the Mississippi State research project concludes in four years. That doesn't seem like an unrealistic desire. After all, Jacobson remembers an older buck that survived several seasons in a heavily hunted public area, despite the fact that all bucks were legal game there.

"During a baiting study we did a couple of years ago, our cameras took photographs of a buck we had tagged during an even earlier study," Jacobson said. "During the second year of that transmitter's life, we lost contact with the buck. We assumed he had been shot and

If you don't take the big bucks like this one, they may die of old age.

carried off. But then we did that baiting study --when he was 5 years old -- and he showed up again. We hadn't seen him for three years. Our cameras took his picture almost every night at the bait. His transmitter-collar was still attached. But I don't know if he is still alive today or not."

Rongstad likes to tell about a 10.5-year-old buck that he radio-tracked across the property of a <u>Deer</u> <u>&</u> <u>Deer</u> <u>Hunting</u> editor a couple of seasons ago. It especially tickled Rongstad that the editor was hunting on his 320-acre parcel while the buck traveled back and forth across it. As far as Rongstad knows, no one ever killed the buck.

Bucks like that conceivably can survive anywhere in the United States. Certainly you will find fewer of these survivors on heavily hunted areas. Still, every year some amazingly superior buck sneaks through the intense hunting pressure.

Even though we may not see them, research strongly indicates these monster-sized, older bucks are out there. They may be more common and closer than you think.

CHAPTER 3

SELECT THE BEST STAND SITE FOR MONSTER-SIZED BUCKS

You can't bag a buck if you don't see the animal. The key to seeing more bucks on every hunt is knowing how to choose the most productive stand sites. Many hunters choose their stand sites using too little information. Perhaps the best way to find a stand site for deer is to utilize the same procedure you use to find your seat at a football game.

Stadium Seats for Bucks

According to Bo Pitman, owner and operator of White Oak Plantation near Tuskegee, Alabama, and longtime hunting guide, ''An aerial photo is like having a ticket to get into a stadium for a football game. On an aerial photo, you can look at how the ground lies. Each piece of property is different, and you'll have to hunt it differently. Also with an aerial photo, you can identify the road systems to enter and leave where you're hunting, the natural barriers, property lines, bodies of water, large fields and funnels.

''You even can distinguish between pine woods and hardwood sites on an aerial photo. The textures of the two types of trees will appear different. Hardwoods will be small, round, blob-looking things on an aerial, since you're actually seeing the tops of the trees. Pine trees will have a smoother texture to them.''

Pitman, who also uses topographical maps to pinpoint land changes where he hunts, terms topographical maps as how he locates the section of the stadium where his ticket should allow him to sit.

"After I study aerial photos to get me into the land, then I use topo maps to help me find the very best places to hunt on that property," Pitman continued. "On topo maps, I look for ridges, valleys and terrain breaks. However, the problem associated with using topo maps is they often are not up-to-date. Usually aerial photos are shot more frequently and contain more up-to-date information. In the Southeast where I primarily hunt, one year a field may be planted in cotton, and three years later loblolly pine 10 feet tall may grow there.

"But to find the row and seat that is the best seat at a football game, which is similar to determining where the most productive place is for me to sit to bag a big buck, I'll have to begin as soon as deer season is over to check the ground. I'll walk carefully over the spots I've located on the aerial photos and the topo maps and look for shed antlers. These antlers will give me an idea of how many and what size of bucks are still on the property. Also I can find where the deer are bedding and feeding and pinpoint their rutting trails.

"Although you can wait until summer to do this on-the-ground scouting, I feel I'm more successful when I scout immediately after deer season ends. Too, in the summer you have to contend with spiderwebs, snakes and dense undergrowth when you're trying to find the best seat in the stadium for your stand site.

"I choose all my stand sites for the next season as though I plan to bowhunt from them. I want the stands to be close to where I expect the deer to appear. Also I pick the most direct route to travel to and from my stand site. Then I don't disturb the deer in the area."

Public Land Stands

Since Pitman hunts on private land, he can be sure the research he does after the season will pay off during the following season. Pitman does not have to consider the people factor that can ruin all your scouting plans if you hunt on public lands.

I always plan for someone else to be at my stand site each time I hunt deer. I assume if I have found a good stand site for deer, so has someone else. I try to find the most productive stand site in relationship to what I know other hunters will do.

You may have to endure the cold and the wet in thick cover to find and take big bucks.

A few years ago I hunted primarily on public lands. While pre-season scouting, I discovered an acorn-producing white oak tree. A huge number of droppings, tracks and hulls of acorns that had been eaten were on the ground as well as nuts that had just fallen from the trees. Two trails led to the white oak tree. I started to lay my game plan.

I determined the best spot to hunt would be within 50 yards of the white oak tree. Then I could watch bucks coming down both trails and have the best opportunity to see the most deer in this area. I thought the second best stand site would be 50 to 100 yards away from the tree down the most well-defined trail. My last choice would be to take a stand on the more dim trail that apparently had not been used very much but still led to the oak tree.

Because I consider myself an average hunter, I believe this way is how the ordinary hunter thinks. But to bag a trophy buck in high-pressure regions, you must out-hunt the average hunters.

When I rethought my original stand site priorities and considered what the other hunters in the area probably would do, I realized some important factors affecting the selection of the best stand sites.

Stand Site I

The white oak tree itself was an obvious feeding hotspot. Any hunter who had scouted the region at all would have drawn this same conclusion. The ground beneath this tree had all the indications that deer would appear there. Since so much obvious sign lay beneath the tree, I knew this spot would be the first place another hunter would choose to hunt. Therefore, I eliminated Stand Site I from my stand site consideration.

Stand Site II

An experienced woodsman rarely will take a stand at the point where he expects the buck to appear to feed, bed or cross a stream. He usually will set up a stand down the trail he supposes the buck will travel to reach that specific location. An experienced hunter also will assume a novice hunter will take a stand close to the feeding site, like the white oak tree. To out-hunt the novice, he will take a stand on the well-defined trail leading to the white oak tree in hopes of bagging the buck before the other hunter sees it. I realized I must eliminate this stand site also.

Stand Site III

I decided to follow the more dim trail 200 to 300 yards away from the white oak tree. My experience had been that older age-class bucks, usually the biggest bucks on the property, rarely utilized the same trail as does and younger age-class bucks traveled to get to a food source, except during the rut. Often an older buck's trail would not be as well-defined as a doe or a younger buck's trail was.

For a buck to sport a rack like this, he must dodge hunters for at least three or four years.

Another factor that made the third trail the best choice was the wind in my section of the country usually blew from the northwest. Since this trail came to the white oak tree from the northwest, I knew that more than likely on the days I hunted, the wind would be in my face and carry my human odor back to the food tree, which would stop most deer from coming to the tree. Too, the wind would blow my human odor directly across the well-defined trail, which would keep any deer from moving down that trail. Probably these deer would funnel onto the trail where I hunted.

On opening morning of the season, I sat in my stand before daylight. I could hear a hunter on the well-defined trail go up a tree with his portable climber just before daylight. As the first rays of light pierced through the dark canopy of leaves above, I saw a fine 8-point buck cautiously coming down the dimly marked trail. I picked up the buck in my Nikon scope. When the crosshairs settled just ahead of the deer's front shoulder, I squeezed the trigger. The buck never moved out of his tracks.

With as much hunting pressure as you find today in most parts of the nation, you not only must be aware of how to hunt deer but also must become very conscious of out-competing other hunters for those deer. The most critical key for becoming a better deer hunter and being more successful when hunting high pressure bucks is tree stand placement. You never must assume that the obvious site will be the most productive place to hunt for nice-sized bucks.

Greenfield Stand Sites

The most obvious greenfield stand site is on or near a trail that comes from the woods to the greenfield. The best time to hunt this stand is late in the afternoon when the deer move to the greenfield to feed. Since many hunters know that information, most of them hunt there.

The second best stand site in a greenfield will be 50 to 100 yards down the trail that leads to the greenfield where you find some type of browse the deer can feed on before they enter the greenfield. Usually many greenfield hunters already will have found this location.

Instead, go past this point further down the trail to where you find two or three other trails intersecting the main trail leading to the greenfield. All the deer that use a particular trail to enter a greenfield don't stay on that trail all the time. They generally come from other trails and other regions to reach that main trail entering the greenfield.

The more experienced deer hunter will look for those trail heads -- often 200 to 400 yards away from the greenfield -- where several trails come together on the main trail leading to the greenfield. Near that intersection of trails is where I prefer to place my tree stand. I want to go to that stand site in the middle of the day.

Most other hunters will take a stand about 1:30 or 2:00 p.m. after lunch on the edge of the greenfield or 100 yards down the trail where the bucks stage before they enter the greenfield. If any bucks are in the greenfield in the middle of the day when these hunters go to their stands, more than likely they will spook those deer out of the field and down the trail where I sit. By hunting well behind the other two hunters who are taking stands on the edge of the greenfield or down the main trail leading

If you know the escape trails that trophy bucks use when they leave thick cover and take a stand there, you may get a shot.

to the greenfield, I make sure I see the bucks that come to the greenfield before the other two hunters do. Also by my being further away from the greenfield, the chances of my seeing a buck in the woods before dark are much better than if I hunt closer to the greenfield.

Escape Trails

If you hunt high-pressure areas, one of the most consistent stand sites you can hunt is escape trails. By assuming the buck you want to take will be spooked by other hunters before you see him, you often can pre-predict where you should hunt as hunting pressure builds.

Whitetail escape trails usually will lead out of or into thick cover. These spots will be near or close to open woodlots, greenfields or agricultural crops. To locate a productive escape trail to hunt over, determine where a buck should be during daylight hours as any other hunter will. Then assume that that deer will be spooked.

If you were the deer, where would you run to get away from the hunter in the shortest time and be able to move into thick cover where the hunter couldn't see you? Or, how could you put some type of natural barrier between you and the hunter like a mountain, a thicket, a creek or a swamp?

The secret to finding the best stand site on an escape trail is to look for the trail coming away from whatever barrier the buck probably has put between him and the hunter. For instance, on a main road with a large, open, wooded area with a thicket on the backside of the open woods, instead of taking a stand on the front side of the thicket where the buck will enter the thick cover, go to the backside of the thicket. Look then for the escape trail coming out of the thick cover where

35

probably the biggest buck will appear. When picking a stand site on an escape trail, always pinpoint the spot where the deer leaves the barrier he uses to put protection between him and the hunter.

If you hunt a hardwood bottom with flooded timber in it, cross the water, and get on the opposite bank from where hunting pressure will come before daylight. As the hunters begin to move into the woods, the deer often will spook, run through the hardwood bottom, enter the flooded timber and move out on the other side where you have your stand. Often when a deer appears on the backside of a barrier, it will walk slowly, will be less nervous and less likely to spot you and usually will present a better shot than if you attempt to stand on the front side of the escape barrier.

Water Stands

To bag a big buck, you must be in a place where the deer least expect to see you at a time of day when the buck doesn't anticipate encountering a hunter. Most of us don't hunt out in the water, because we're more interested in keeping our feet dry and hunting deer with the least possible amount of hassle.

However, to take an older, monster-sized buck, you must work for them. To determine where an exceptional tree stand site is for trophy bucks, study the area you hunt. Search for spots where no one will want to put a tree stand. Learn how to reach that place without being seen and how to leave without disturbing any evidence to let others know you've been in the region.

I particularly like a tree stand site over water in river bottom drainages. Two different methods will aid you to access a water stand. You can buddy-hunt using a small boat, or you can wear waders.

If an oxbow lake, a beaver pond or a backwater slough is close to where you are hunting, use some type of portable boat or canoe to get you and your partner's tree stands to the places to set up. Paddle to a tree standing out in the water. Have your hunting friend lock on his tree stand, climb the tree and attach his safety belt once he is up the tree.

Then you paddle to the second stand site, pull the boat onshore, hide the boat under brush or bushes and wade out to your tree stand site wearing either hip or thigh-high waders and carrying your tree stand. After the hunt is over and you come out of your stand, retrieve the boat, and pick up the other hunter.

Taking a stand on the edge of water may allow you to see a trophy buck move through that water.

By using this strategy, you ...

 * leave no scent in the area you plan to hunt,

 * can watch the water's edge, which most often is a natural deer migration route -- especially if acorns float on the edge of the water,

 * will surprise the deer, since they don't expect to see hunters in trees over water,

 * will find other hunters coming to hunt that region often will drive deer to you if they come by land,

 * can load any deer you bag into the boat or canoe and transport it out easily to your vehicle.

Even if you don't have access to a portable boat or a small canoe, you can wear hip or chest waders to move out into the water well away from the bank and place your tree stand to hunt.

One of my favorite stands to hunt in a beaver swamp late in the season is in flooded timber. These regions will be full of white oak and red oak acorns. When the rains come in late December and the beaver pond overflows its banks, the acorns that have been on the forest floor float to the surface.

On one morning, I had reached my stand before first light and was in my tree stand about an hour before the area had enough light to shoot. In the stillness of the morning, I could hear woodducks whistling through the trees and splashing in the beaver slough as they landed. I also heard the noisy quacking of mallard ducks dropping into the standing timber and feeding on the floating acorns.

As the light increased, dripping water and popping nuts were the loudest sounds in the area. Immediately I knew deer were feeding out in the water, possibly along the water's edge. Using my Nikon Naturalist binoculars, I looked for the deer. I preferred using these bigger, heavier binoculars because they seemed brighter than the more compact binoculars and gave me the advantage of spotting deer sooner when the light was still low.

Looking through the mist rising from the swamp, I saw four does knee-deep in the water feeding on the acorns. Behind the does, I spotted another deer with his head behind a big cypress tree. When a woodduck flew into the swamp like a World War II fighter pilot and splashed not 20 yards from the deer standing near the cypress, the animal jerked its head back. I saw a flash of ivory.

I studied the buck in my binoculars. Although he only was a 6 point, his antlers stood wide and looked heavy. Because a breeze blew from the shore out across the beaver pond, I knew the deer couldn't smell me. I waited for a better shot. When the second woodduck flew in and landed in the same area as the first woodduck, the 6 point backed away from the cypress tree and fed down the slough toward me.

The buck stopped between two sweet gum trees and presented a front shoulder shot. As the crosshairs found the spot I was searching for, I squeezed the trigger. At the explosion of the rifle, ducks took to the air, and does splashed down the slough. However, the 6 point lay in the water where he last had stood.

That same water stand site produced nice-sized bucks for me six out of the eight years I hunted that property. I never saw another hunter in that part of the woods.

Tree stand placement is critical to whitetail success. Once you learn to carefully scout after studying topo maps and aerial photos, discard the obvious, and determine what a deer will do before he does it, you will be more consistent in placing your stand where you can take a trophy buck.

CHAPTER 4

CACKLE UP A BIG BUCK

The 9-point buck stood looking from the left to the right for a full two minutes. Only 20 yards away, he presented an easy shot. He'd come to the cackling sound of the Lohman's grunt tube my deer hunting guide, Chris Yeoman of Rapid City, South Dakota, used. On this hunt, I'd already seen three bucks much bigger than the 9 point in this same area. I sat motionless in the snow under the cedars and watched the buck walk off.

Five minutes later when Yeoman, who also is a turkey hunting guide, once again cackled on the grunt tube, I heard a crashing in the cedars to my left. As I turned, I watched a 6-point whitetail walk to within 30 yards, offer a shot and then move away. Yeoman cackled one more time, but no other deer appeared. After moving 250 yards down through the cedars on the edge of the creek, we cackled in a 4-point buck. From these experiences, I'm convinced that cackling in bucks is the most deadly big-buck deer-calling technique I've ever used.

Why Cackle

I originally learned to cackle for bucks from Wayne Carlton of Montrose, Colorado, president of Carlton Calls, who told me, ''The cackling grunt is a way to call deer much like cackling and cutting calls in turkey gobblers. This particular call is much faster than the usual grunt call, has more excitement in the call and simulates the deer's movement.''

When you need to get a big buck in really close for a shot with your bow, try cackling -- (Drawing by Jim Tostrud).

Carlton taught me to cackle when we bowhunted. Carlton had cackled in a nice 8 point earlier and arrowed him with his Bear First Strike bow. That afternoon, he took me into the woods and demonstrated the call to me.

"Most deer hunters call bucks with three, slow, rather long grunts, wait 15 minutes and then give the same series of grunts again," Carlton explained. "But if a buck walks through the area where you're calling and he doesn't hear you grunt, then you won't be able to call him in to where you wait. By calling more, you increase your odds for more bucks hearing and coming to your calls. From watching bucks and does, I've noticed when they're really excited, they grunt almost continuously."

If the three grunts most hunters make can be described in Morse Code, they will be three long dashes. The cackling call Carlton gives on his grunt tube is much shorter and more staccato and will look more like a series of 20 to 30 dots in Morse Code instead of three, long dashes. At the same time Carlton gives these short, fast grunts, he takes the tube end of the call, points it starting from his left toward the ground and then as he grunts moves it around the tree where he's taking a stand.

"I'm throwing the call like a turkey hunter cups his hand over his mouth when he's using a diaphragm call and throws his call from left to right or right to left out in front of himself," Carlton said. "By throwing the call toward the ground when I'm in a tree stand, the buck hears the sound coming from the ground instead of the tree, which is more natural. By moving the call around the tree, the call sounds like a buck walks or runs around a tree chasing a doe."

Besides giving a faster moving call when Carlton cackles to bucks, he extends and collapses the tube at the same time he moves the call around the tree.

"Both bucks and does grunt," Carlton reported. "When I extend the tube, I get a deep grunt like that given by a buck. When I collapse the tube, I make a higher pitched grunt, like the sound made by a doe. Therefore, by extending and collapsing the tube as I move it out in front of me, I imitate the sound and movement of a buck chasing a doe and both of them grunting."

Carlton is quick to explain he is not the father of the cackling-to-bucks idea. Carlton has combined the strategies of several people who have been using this call effectively for years.

How to Cackle

Rob Keck and Carl Brown, both executives with the National Wild Turkey Federation in Edgefield, South Carolina, have utilized this cackling call successfully on deer for more than 10 years.

Calling aggressively on the grunt call can bring a big buck in on the run.

"Although the wild turkey and the white-tailed deer are two completely different animals, they do have some similarities that made me believe that some of the techniques I used for turkey calling would be productive in calling deer," Keck recalled.

"Both the wild turkey and the whitetail become extremely active during the breeding season. Their No. 1 purpose in life during that time is to breed females of their species. They both become very territorially minded. They will come to calling that simulates another male's intruding into their territory and trying to breed their females or sounds like a female that's ready to breed. During the rut, calling excites deer more than at any other time of the year."

Keck had noticed from watching deer in clearcuts and big timber areas that bucks often moved through the region where he was calling in less than two minutes. He realized if he only called every 15 minutes, numbers of bucks would pass within hearing distance that he wouldn't be able to call in utilizing his grunt tube.

When you cackle in bucks, deer usually will come on the run. Have your gun up, and be ready to take the shot.

"The only way a call can be productive is for the deer to hear it, which means you need to call more," Keck commented. "If you use the cackling call prior to, during and just after the rut when the buck is most easily excited, then your chances of calling him in to where you are drastically increases. In one morning of hunting, I have called in eight to 15 bucks using this tactic. Most of the time, the bucks that come to the cackle call are the older, bigger, trophy-sized bucks."

Besides hunting with Brown and Keck, another instance that helped Wayne Carlton develop this philosophy of cackling in bucks occurred when Carlton visited Dr. Keith Causey, professor of Wildlife Science at Auburn University in Auburn, Alabama.

"I was filming deer at Auburn and recording the sounds they made," Carlton said, "I noticed when a buck chased a doe, I could hear his internal organs bounce as he ran.

43

"The grunt the buck makes when he runs is short and broken rather than a long, steady grunt like most hunters use to grunt in deer. Many hunters use the words 'tending grunt' to describe the three, slow, grunt calls they give during the breeding season to attempt to call in bucks. Bucks do make this sound when they're standing or walking slowly behind does. But when bucks chase does, they give short and choppy grunts because of the bouncing of their internal organs as they run."

To get a better perspective of why this cackling call is so effective with bucks, try to jog and sing at the same time. You'll notice as you sing, the words are broken when your feet pound the ground. When a buck hears a broken grunt and the grunt call moving around a tree, he may believe another excited buck in his area is chasing an estrous doe. That estrous doe may provide the second buck an opportunity to breed if he can get to her.

If the dominant buck hears this call, then he'll come in quickly not only to breed but also to defend his harem of does and run the intruder out of his territory. Even a subordinate buck will respond to this call because he hopes the buck running the doe may be subordinate to him.

"I experimented with deer calling and learned by combining the cackling grunt call with rattling antlers that I greatly increased the number of bucks I was seeing," Carl Brown explained. "I found that many of the types of calls I used for turkeys could be incorporated into my deer calling.

"However, one of the differences between calling turkeys and calling deer is when you give an excited call to a gobbler, he usually will answer you with a call. But bucks won't call back to you. You can't know how productive a call is until you actually spot the deer. Therefore, you have to believe in the call and continue to use it until you see the buck."

When Bucks Hear Cackling

Bucks that respond to a call generally come in to where you are in one of two ways.

"There are crashers and sneakers," Rob Keck mentioned. "Some bucks will come on the run when they hear cackling -- crashing through the woods as they approach your stand. Other bucks will sneak into your stand, and you'll never hear them. They'll just appear in front of you."

When you cackle to bucks, they'll either come in quickly or sneak in slowly -- (Drawing by Kelli Breland).

Although no one truly understands what a buck thinks when he hears this cackling grunt, many speculate that by changing the tone and the pitch of the call as you call aggressively and throwing the sound to the ground and around your stand that the deer hears more and different sounds, any of which may lure in a buck.

"We know from turkey hunting that sometimes you must use a wide variety of calls to bring in a gobbler," Brown said. "Often a gobbler only will come to one of those calls on the day you're calling. I think deer respond to calls in a similar way. A buck may come more to the grunt when the tube is collapsed and giving a high-pitched grunt than he will on other days when he may respond to the deeper sound produced by extending the tube."

Even though Carlton, Brown and Keck all agree that cackling to bucks is most effective just before, during and after the breeding season, Carlton utilizes this method to call bucks in the early bow season even when no scraping or rutting activity is occurring.

"Cackling in the early season brings in bucks because the call sounds like more than one deer in an area," Carlton explained. "Because deer are social animals, a buck will want to come and associate with the other deer he hears grunting. If a buck hears more than one deer calling from the same spot, I believe he feels that region is safe to enter."

To work a buck that has responded to the cackling grunt call but stops short of bow range, Carlton recommends you, "Turn the call around, and suck in on the tube part of the call. By reversing the call, you can give a softer grunt and a calmer grunt than you can by blowing through the other end of the call.

"Also by putting the call in my left breast pocket with the tube end of the call out, I simply can drop my chin and suck in on the tube end of the call. I have my hands free to draw and shoot when the buck comes in closer. Because the sound of the call is muffled, the buck has a more difficult time distinguishing where the sound's coming from and is less likely to spot me in my tree stand."

How much more productive is the cackling grunt for luring in bucks than the traditional call of making three, slow grunts and waiting 15 minutes? According to Rob Keck and Carl Brown, they have doubled or perhaps tripled the number of bucks they see by using the cackling grunt. Wayne Carlton has found he calls in both more and bigger bucks with a cackling grunt.

The art of calling deer is evolving much like turkey calling has evolved. Twenty years ago, the traditional way to call turkeys was to cluck three times, yelp three times and then not call again for 30 to 40 minutes. The cackle call wasn't well known at that time, and very few people tried to excite gobblers to get them to come in to where the hunters were. But a new breed of turkey hunters started experimenting with calling techniques and learned that cutting, cackling and giving excited calls could increase the number of turkeys they lured in and bring the birds in faster.

Today some of the nation's best turkey callers have applied the cackle call to their deer hunting. The cackling grunt has caused deer hunters to rethink the way they call and signals a new wave of interest in deer-calling strategies.

CHAPTER 5

SHOOT TROPHY BUCKS
ON THE RUN

"How well can you shoot, John?" Chris Yeoman of Rapid City, South Dakota, a deer hunting guide and good friend, asked me.

That's like asking someone, "How pretty is your wife?" If you don't think she's the best-looking woman you've ever seen, then why would you have married her? And if you don't think you're a good shot, then why would you be out hunting? "Well, from 0 to 100 yards, I believe I can stand toe-to-toe with most hunters," I answered.

"But how good are you at 300 to 500 yards taking running deer?" Yeoman questioned.

I thought Yeoman was joking, but he was as serious as a hanging judge. I learned later that Yeoman and his hunting buddy, Dr. Jim Nelson, also from Rapid City, consistently bagged trophy bucks at these distances.

Nelson takes two or three deer a season in several states. Seventy percent of the bucks Nelson bags he downs as the animals run at 100 to 500 yards away.

This type of long-distance shooting and hunting is as foreign to me as an alien from outer space is. In the Southeast, where I spend much of my deer-hunting time, a long shot is 150 yards. In the woods and fields of the East, rarely can you see a deer at a much greater distance.

But in the wide open spaces of the West, long-distance shooting is a way of life. The men who consistently take the older-age bucks with the wide racks and high tines have learned to shoot accurately at distances that stagger an Easterner's mind.

How They Learn to Shoot

One of the reasons Jim Nelson, Chris Yeoman and many of the riflemen of the West regularly make these unbelievable shots at running deer is because from the time they're young they shoot coyotes. Yeoman and Nelson hunt coyotes intensively. For several years, Yeoman even was a professional coyote hunter.

"I used a Lohman's predator call for the coyotes," Yeoman recalled. "At one time, you could make good money calling and taking coyotes. But the market for coyote pelts has been depressed in recent years."

In one season, Yeoman called and bagged 52 coyotes. Of those 52 animals, 20 of them were taken on the run.

"I also missed about 50 coyotes that year," Yeoman remembered with a chuckle. "We shoot a lot of ammunition when we're coyote hunting. When you hunt this open country where you can see a long way and have the opportunity to shoot at great distances, the more ammunition you shoot, the better shot you'll become. Another advantage when hunting running coyotes is if you miss the critter, you can see where your bullet hits and still have time to try another shot. For instance, if you shoot behind the animal, on the next shot, you can swing further ahead of it and usually compensate."

"We shoot numbers of coyotes on the run at 100 to 300 yards," Nelson explained. "The coyotes are much smaller than deer. As you build up your confidence at shooting coyotes at long distances, you have every reason to believe you can make that same kind of shot at a deer."

How Nelson Took Two Bucks on the Run

The two weeks before I arrived in South Dakota, Nelson already had bagged two bucks, one that scored 158-1/8 Boone & Crockett points and another that scored 170-1/8 B & C. Both of these deer were taken on the run at more than 200 yards. The first deer Nelson let one of his hunting partners, Delana Russell, try to bag. But Delana missed the deer three times before the buck went into a drainage. Nelson and

When a big buck like this one breaks from thick cover, you've got to know how to aim and shoot accurately -- (Drawing by Jim Tostrud).

his party moved into a small, thick-cover area and jumped not only that buck but another big buck and 10 other deer.

"The deer came out of the drainage, running full-out and almost straightaway from us," Nelson reported. "But since they angled a little to the right, I knew I wouldn't have a very difficult shot.

"When the deer were at about 250 yards running down a fenceline, I aimed at the biggest buck's nose and squeezed the trigger. The deer only ran 100 yards before he piled up. The bullet had gone into the back side of the animal's flank and continued on straight up into the lungs, bringing him down."

Two weeks earlier Nelson bagged one of the biggest bucks he'd ever taken. This deer was also running almost straightaway.

"Normally I would aim for the back of the deer's head," Nelson mentioned. "However, on this particular shot, I knew the bullet probably would land somewhat off to the right if I aimed at the back of the buck's head, because of the angle he was running away. Then I'd miss him. Instead, I aimed for the tip of the deer's nose. When I squeezed the trigger, the bullet hit him in the center of the neck, and the big buck tumbled.

"When you're shooting big deer at long distances, you've got to have a steady rest, you must take your time, and you must know exactly where to aim. Even then you can't be absolutely sure where the bullet will land. But from past experience, you can predict where you should hit the animal. In both these cases, I didn't doubt that I could make the shots."

Where to Aim

When Nelson shoots at a deer running straightaway at 200 to 300 yards, he first will take a kneeling, sitting or prone position.

"You must make sure you've got a solid rest," Nelson said. "You must steady a rifle to shoot it accurately at long distances."

Nelson usually sits and steadies his rifle on his knee or lies on the ground in the prone position, although Yeoman prefers to use a forked stick to brace his rifle and steady for the shot.

"With the stick, I not only can steady my rifle, but I still can swing on a level plane with the deer. I usually carry a forked stick. I've learned I can shoot more accurately with the stick than I can when I'm either sitting or lying down."

When either man takes the shot, he aims for the back of the deer's head and expects the bullet to land either in the buck's neck or shoulder region, depending on how fast the deer's moving and at what angle the deer is going away from him.

According to Nelson, one of the worst shots is a broadside shot. "The distance you must lead the deer to bring him down when he's running broadside to you is amazing. If the buck's only 100 yards out, you can aim in front of him and generally get a shoulder shot. But if the

Chris Yeoman, pictured here, is a master at long-distance shooting for deer.

buck's running 200 to 300 yards broadside to me, I usually lead him 10 to 15 feet -- a distance that is difficult to judge when the deer is moving.

"I aim at the deer and begin to swing in front of him just like I do when I'm swinging on ducks. As I continue to swing in front of the deer, I squeeze the trigger. But this shot is not a good one to make. However, one of the advantages of hunting in open country is that in many instances you can see where the bullet lands just like you can when you're hunting coyotes. Then, when you take your next shot, you can adjust your swing before you squeeze the trigger."

"At 200 to 300 yards, when a deer runs broadside to you, your chances are far greater at missing it than if it's running straightaway from you at that distance," Yeoman observed. "Aim like you're shooting ducks. Begin your swing behind the deer, pick the deer up in your riflescope, and continue to float and swing in front of the deer before squeezing the trigger.

"At these distances, you can't hold the crosshairs out in front of the deer. Let him run into the crosshairs, and shoot accurately. You have to swing with and then past the target, squeeze the trigger and continue your swing. This shot is one of the most difficult for most hunters to learn to make. This shot is more like shotgun shooting or wingshooting than rifle shooting. Another reason this shot is hard to make is that most hunters really can't believe how fast and how far deer can move from the time they squeeze their triggers until their bullets land.''

Both hunters agree the easiest shot to make on a running deer is when the animal is running straightaway.

"When the deer's running away from you, you have the full length of the animal to hit," Nelson commented. "If you hold on the head area, you'll have a good chance of taking him."

One of the reasons Nelson can shoot so accurately at great distances is because he's shooting a Remington Model 700 .25-06.

"I like this gun because it's fast and flat-shooting, and at 300 yards, I'm dead on," Nelson said. "I set my gun 3 inches high at 100 yards, and I can aim dead on from 400 yards down to 100 yards or less."

How to Hunt Uphill and Downhill

Another factor that determines your aiming point when you're trying to take a buck that's running away from you is whether he's running uphill or downhill.

"If the deer runs uphill, you increase the lead past his nose," Nelson said. "You have to aim a little more in front of him than if he's running downhill. If the deer's running downhill, then you may not have to increase the lead at all, because the deer will run down into the bullet.

"One of the problems associated with trying to teach someone to accurately take deer on the run is that your system of aiming has to become instinctive. From shooting hundreds of coyotes over many years, you learn how to vary your lead depending on the grade the animal is going up or down. The steeper the grade, the more you may have to change your lead from when a deer is running on flat ground straight away from you. At lesser grades, your lead will change less.

"This problem is the same one hunters have shooting ducks or geese. To be accurate, they must calculate in their minds where the birds will be when the shot arrives. Because rifles shoot at such great speeds, we often tend to forget that even at the speed the bullet's traveling, the bullet can't land where you're aiming when the animal's moving away from you. By the time the bullet arrives where the deer was when you squeezed the trigger, the deer has left that spot. Most hunters miss running deer because they don't lead them enough."

When you push big bucks out of thick cover, often the largest buck will be the last buck in the herd.

Of the 13 deer Nelson has mounted on his walls, seven were bagged on the run. Nelson and Yeoman also take so many trophy bucks because they study the terrain. They look for small pockets where big bucks hide out, and they drive those pockets to flush the deer from cover. When a trophy comes out into the open, he's usually moving quickly and will rarely stop. To take this buck, you must shoot quickly and accurately.

What Guns, Bullets and Scopes Are Best

Besides gaining experience by shooting coyotes at long distances, both Yeoman and Nelson believe their combinations of rifles, scopes and bullets are critical to their success. The rifles Yeoman and Nelson recommend for this kind of shooting are those that push the bullet out at velocities over 3,000-feet/second.

"The .25-06, .270, and .300 Win. Mag. are my favorite calibers," Yeoman explained. "Each caliber has its favorite bullet, which is determined by the bullet's length and ballistic coefficient -- the ease at which the bullet goes through the air. In the .25-06, the 100-grain bullet seems best. Jim prefers the factory-loaded Hornady 100-grain bullet. In the .300 Win. Mag. I shoot, the 180-grain bullet seems to be the best."

Yeoman likes either a Nosler partition or a Barnes-X bullet.

"Both of these bullets are excellent big game bullets with tremendous knock-down power," Yeoman reported. "I like to shoot the solid-copper Barnes-X because of the way the bullet mushrooms into an X-shape. This bullet also has the ability to retain all its weight since only the front portion of the bullet actually mushrooms. This action produces tremendous knockdown power at long distances.''

The gun's ability to shoot flat over a long distance and deliver a bullet that can bring a running deer down quickly is why Nelson shoots a .25-06 and Yeoman likes the .300 Win. Both of these calibers are efficient at taking moving game at great distances. Just as important as the rifle and the bullet are to Yeoman and Nelson's success, each man knows the riflescope he uses also plays a major role in his ability to shoot accurately over long distances.

Why Use High-Magnification Scopes

Both men prefer higher magnification when shooting deer at long range.

''I like the 4-12X Leupold scope,'' Nelson said. ''I like to use the 12X to judge the buck's rack quickly at 200 to 300 yards. When you have a buck running away from you at that distance, you don't have enough time to take your binocular, study the buck, make a decision whether or not you should shoot, lower the binocular, mount your rifle, find the deer in your scope and take the shot. By having the ability to zoom out to 12X, I can check out the rack. Then, if I need to back the scope down to hold steadier and shoot accurately, I can. But all these adjustments can be made quickly and easily by having this type of scope.''

Another advantage the 4-12X Leupold offers Nelson is that because he hunts the thick-cover areas, he can set his scope on 4X. If he sees the buck in thick cover before it breaks to run, Nelson can make the shot quickly and easily at close range with the lesser power. Once the deer breaks from cover and begins to run away from Nelson, he can zoom the scope up and make long-distance running shots. Nelson can find running bucks in his scope even at long distance and even with the scope at 12X because he has spent the time required to set his eye relief properly.

''One of the reasons I like the Leupold scope is because you have far more eye relief -- 2 to 4-1/2 inches -- than you do with some other scopes,'' Nelson explained. ''Being able to rapidly find that deer in

To take a really nice buck like this one, using a man-drive may be your best option.

your scope is important when you're shooting at long distances. I can look over the top of my scope and see the buck as he's running away. Then, when I bring my cheek down to the stock, I can see the deer in my scope between the crosshairs.

"When some hunters look at a deer running away from then over their scopes, and when they look through their scopes, they can't find

Taking an offhand shot at a running buck will require more luck than skill to maintain accuracy. However, if you use a tripod to support your gun or get in a prone position, you drastically will increase your odds.

it. Then they have to search for the buck and waste valuable aiming time.

"If I could make one suggestion to improve a hunter's ability to take bucks on the run, it would be to make sure you first purchase a scope with good eye relief. Next get the scope mounted so that when you look over the scope and bring your cheek down, you don't lose track of the target."

Another advantage to utilizing the 12X scope is when Nelson aims at a deer running away from him he has more animal in his scope to aim at than if his scope is set on a lesser power.

"With the scope set on 12X, at 100 to 200 yards I see just crosshairs and deer in the scope, and aiming is much easier and faster," Nelson said. "If you've got the scope at a lesser power, you have more terrain and less deer at which to aim. The possibility of your shooting more accurately when you've got a buck on the run is better with a higher powered scope. Add to this factor a kneeling or a sitting position where

Field glasses and/or high-powered scopes are vital to the trophy hunter.

your hold is more stable, and you double or triple your chances of shooting accurately."

In South Dakota, where Nelson primarily hunts, 200-yard-plus shots are common. He is convinced the larger-powered scopes play a major role in his shooting accuracy.

Most People Shouldn't Attempt Long Running Shots

Yeoman has taken running deer at distances out to 500 yards. Both Yeoman and Nelson consistently bag deer on the run from 200 to 400 yards.

"To be able to shoot accurately at great distances, you have to do a lot of shooting at moving targets," Yeoman explained. "But just because you can shoot accurately at a moving target that's further than 100 yards doesn't mean you should take a shot at a running deer at that distance.

"Most hunters don't have the right types of guns or the correct bullets to bag deer at that distance. I've seen hunters come to the West with 7mm Mags and hollow-point bullets and try to make one of those long-distance running shots. The problem is not in their ability to possibly hit the deer but rather what occurs if they do hit the deer. They'll often get poor hits without proper penetration. Most likely they'll wound animals that may get away.

"When I shoot, I'm not simply attempting to hit the buck. I want to take him with a bullet placed in his vital organs that will bring him down quickly and efficiently. Usually that's where my bullet will land.

"But Jim and I can shoot accurately because we've got the rifles, scopes, bullets and the experience to make those long-distance running shots. To regularly take bucks on the run, you've got to shoot a lot of ammunition at a large number of targets."

These two men's long-range shooting skills have developed to where they now are automatic responses. Nelson and Yeoman don't have to think how to aim and when to squeeze their triggers. Instead their brains automatically make these calculations. Their secrets to shooting big bucks on the run at great distances include using the right equipment, practicing shooting at smaller game and having years of experience.

CHAPTER 6

USE MAN-DRIVES FOR MONSTER-SIZED BUCKS

I was told to go to the edge of the water and take a stand. However, I felt if I stopped 30 yards before I reached the edge of the swamp, then I could spot a buck going between the edge of the water and the hill beside it, walking down the top of the ridge or moving through the bottom on the other side of the hill. By taking a stand in this spot, I thought I was much more likely to see and get a shot at a buck than if I sat on the edge of the water where I only would be able to watch deer moving down that edge.

I heard Donald Spence's hands come together to make a sharp clapping sound. Then I heard movement in the water below me. Wood ducks flushed. As their wings reached upward to latch on hooks of invisible air and catapult their bodies skyward, I saw brown bodies sneaking through the flooded timber. When I spotted a glint of ivory through one of the small openings in the woodlot, I realized I had sat down 30 yards away from an opportunity to bag a buck.

If I had listened to Donald Spence and sat immediately on the edge of the water, I would have had an easy and clean shot at the buck. From where I should have been sitting, the buck would have passed less than 30 yards from me. Because the wind was in my face, the buck would not have smelled me. Although the deer was in the water, the water was

Large man-drives are not nearly as effective as small man-drives.

less than knee-deep. But I made the fatal mistake other hunters have made when hunting with Spence. I tried to second guess this master of the man-drive.

My hunting experience dictated that deer always traveled edges, ridges and hollows. But Spence had predicted the deer would move in the water when he caused them to get up and leave their bedding area. The deer showed up exactly where he knew they would as though he had drawn a map of the hunt. I failed to get a shot.

When I saw Spence approach, I felt like the cat that had been caught with the canary in his mouth as he asked, ''Did you see any deer?'' although he already knew the answer to his question.

''A buck and three does came out in the water exactly where you said they would, but I couldn't see them well enough to take a shot,'' I explained.

Rather than reading me the riot act and telling me that if I just had followed his directions we would have a buck to drag out of the woods, Spence knew I understood that because I had not followed his directions, I had failed to bag my buck. With the wisdom that comes from years of hunting and dealing with hunters, a big grin parted Spence's mouth as he laughed and said, ''Come on, John, we'll go get another one.''

I followed the master of the man-deer drive to another part of the woods. As deadly as rattlesnakes and as silent as panthers, Donald Spence and his wife Jody, of Monticello, Mississippi, move through the woods like ghosts. They can walk a buck right to you and have him stop within easy bow, black-powder or rifle range with the system Spence has developed. The Spences bag several big bucks each season with bows and arrows, black-powder rifles and conventional rifles.

"In my home state of Mississippi, I once drove deer with hounds," Spence recalled. "About two hours into the hunt, the hounds always would take a deer out of hearing. Then all the standers would sit around wishing the dogs would come back, since we had no way to move the deer.

"One day I went down through a thicket to see if I could drive the deer to the standers. Sure enough, a big buck jumped up and ran over the stand line. The hunters took him. I decided I was wasting time waiting on hounds and that I might be able to move deer more effectively by man-driving them rather than driving with dogs."

As Spence developed new and better techniques of man-driving deer, he discovered he could move far more deer than the hounds could. He sold his dogs and perfected a system of driving deer that was deadly effective for him that will produce nice-sized bucks for you.

Know Your Country

The key to a successful man-drive is knowing the land where you plan to drive the deer.

"I like to drive in an area with some type of barrier on one side such as an open field, a creek or a steep mountain," Spence mentioned. "By using this method, the barriers force the deer to the standers. My favorite places to drive are strips of woods between fields, especially thick woods."

Understand How to Drive

Putting on a productive man-drive Donald Spence style means the wind must be in the stander's face and at the driver's back. Then a buck will not smell the standers. Spence uses his human odor, more than the sound he makes, to move the deer through the woods and to the standers.

"I'll zig-zag from one edge of a woodlot to the other edge as I drive," Spence said. "I don't make that much noise as I walk through the woods. I just want the deer to realize somebody is in the woods with them. I don't necessarily want them to know where I am. Occasionally I will tap a tree with a stick, or I'll clap my hands."

Spence has learned that any sharp sound like a stick's breaking, the snapping of branches or clapping your hands startles the hidden deer and causes them to get up and run 10 or 12 yards. Then the deer will stop and look back to see what has made the noise.

"If I hunt thick cover, I may not drive more than 100 to 300 yards because I don't want the deer to be too far out in front of me where the standers can't see them," Spence explained. "In this type of driving, the deer's attention is focused on me. When he sees, hears or smells me, he will move out 10 to 20 yards, stop and then look to see where I am. As the deer pauses, the bowhunter, the black-powder hunter or the rifle hunter can get a clean, still shot at the deer."

When Spence drives open woods, he may put the standers further out in front of him.

"If I drive in the open woods, I try to move through the woods without making a sound," Spence mentioned. "I rely on the deer's being able to see and smell me rather than hear me. Since I'm not walking directly at the deer but rather am moving from side to side, then the deer are not trying to run away from me as much as they are attempting to get out of my way. Generally they will be moving much slower than if I drive straight at them."

Spence does not scream and holler as he goes through the woods because he has learned from dog hunting deer that as long as deer know where the danger is and in what direction it is traveling, they may remain bedded down and let trouble pass them by.

"I've stood in woods before and watched a pack of dogs race through the woods chasing a buck," Spence observed. "After the dogs are out of hearing, the largest bucks in that region will begin to stand up and move around. I'm convinced deer know those dogs are chasing one particular animal and that as long as they remain still, they will not be in danger.

"I believe deer view a driver like a dog. A hunter who goes through the woods screaming, hollering and making a lot of noise like a dog does when he barks and runs through the woods lets the deer pinpoint where the driver is at all times. The deer may just sit still. But when the deer realize a hunter or something is in the woods making a clapping sound

Donald Spence simply breaks sticks as he walks through the woods to make bucks move.

or breaking sticks and are not certain what that something is or where it is, then they will get up, move around and try to stay out of the way.''

Spence has found the deer's inability to know where the driver is is the key to moving more deer.

''Another advantage to this style of man-driving deer is you don't frighten the bucks,'' Spence commented. ''If you scare a buck that runs past the standers, more than likely the standers will not be able to take the deer. I've been on a stand before when Jody has been driving and seen a buck out in front of her, stop and look back at her when she is less than 40 yards from him. As long as the buck can see her, he never will move. One of the problems associated with man- driving is not only being able to move the deer but also being certain you don't move the deer so fast the hunters can't get a shot. Then the drive is ineffective.''

Spence can drive a small head of woods using his clapping, stick-snapping, silent technique for driving, move 500 yards to the next area he wants to hunt and put a drive on there.

"One of the problems with noisy drives where the hunters scream and holler is not only do you spook the deer that are within the drive site, you also spook the deer within 1/2- mile from your drive site," Spence said. "Using this silent strategy and depending on my human odor combined with my snapping, clapping technique, I don't have to move far at all before I begin my second drive."

When one drive is completed, Spence and his standers, which may number from one to four, whisper and determine where the next drive will take place. Very quietly the standers will take their positions, and the next drive will begin. Being quiet, moving quickly and not putting any more pressure on the deer than is absolutely necessary to make the deer move has enabled the Spences and their fellow hunters to bag some nice-sized bucks while putting on from five to 15 drives in a day.

Know When to Drive

Unlike most hunters who try to drive deer at daylight, Donald Spence prefers to wait until 9:00 a.m. or 10:00 a.m.

"If you start the drive too early, the deer still will be up and moving around and won't be in those little thick-cover areas where they normally bed down," Spence advised. "I try to let the deer get into a bedding region and then slowly move from his bedding site to where my stander is. I still hunt for the first hour or two of daylight. Then I begin my man-drive."

Learn How to Place Your Standers

Spence uses the terrain and his knowledge of the woods to determine where he should put standers.

"Any time I spot a deer get up and run off, if I am hunting by myself or with my wife, Jody, I try to follow that deer and see where he is going and how he gets there," Spence reported. "After a rain, trailing and tracking deer is much easier. By following the deer, I learn where his escape routes are and where to put my standers. If I know a trail a deer takes to escape from thick cover, then I will put a stander on it, even if that stander is a half mile away from the next stander."

64

Often the biggest bucks will be in the thickest cover.

When Spence hunts a pine forest where the deer can see great distances, he spaces his standers further apart than if he hunts thick-cover areas.

"If the woods are thick, my standers may be only 100 yards apart," Spence explained. "But if the woods are open, I may have the standers about 500 yards apart." Allowing only a few standers and one or two drivers to participate means you can hunt more property more effectively.

"The more standers you have, the more problems you must deal with," Spence commented. "Somebody always will say, 'I think I ought to stand over there,' or ask, 'I think we should take a lunch break,' or 'Why do I have to stand in this spot instead of that place?' "

To solve the people problems that accompany a deer drive, Spence becomes a benevolent dictator. He has learned the fewer people he has to direct, the more efficiently they all can hunt.

"Although we can cover more area if we have more people, I'm totally convinced we take more bucks with one or two drivers and fewer people who surround smaller woodlots and hunt more efficiently," Spence reported.

Consider the Weather for Driving Bucks

Besides the terrain, Spence allows the weather to dictate what type of area he drives. If the weather is warm, Spence usually will drive open woods since he believes deer prefer to be in the open woods where they can be cooler. In very cold weather, he generally drives thick cover such as briar patches, young pine thickets and/or cedar thickets. He has learned deer use these areas to protect themselves against the cold wind and bad weather.

Use a One-Man Drive

Although the Spences hunt 2700 acres, when they drive together they often will hunt less than six or seven acres. These drives may require less than 30 minutes to put on. The Spences decide who will stand and who will drive. The stander goes to his spot in the woods, and then the driver starts coming to him. Each small head of woods they drive usually will produce some deer.

"To make this tactic work, the stander must get to his or her stand without making any noise or alerting the deer anyone is in the woods," Spence explained. "Then when the driver begins, the only noise and sound the deer hears comes from behind him, which causes the deer to move forward to the stander."

Another reason Donald and Jody Spence are so effective at driving deer is because they hunt the land so frequently they have learned the deer's escape routes.

"If we drive a little woodlot and see a deer but don't get a shot at him and then drive that same woodlot a week later and the deer gets by us using that same escape route, then the next time we drive we know where the deer will go," Spence said. "We will put the stander on that escape trail. Then when we come through the woods driving, the stander usually will bag the buck."

Pinpointing the escape routes deer use to leave thick cover or small woodlots, placing a stander on these escape routes and then creating a disturbance behind the deer makes a two-man drive very productive. By alternating drivers, Spence and his wife each have a time when they sit and wait for the deer as well as a time when they walk and try to spook the deer.

"We rarely will take the same stand more than twice in a season in any area we drive," Spence emphasized. "If you do, then the deer will

Many times a buck will let you walk right past him.

pattern you and understand how to dodge you the next time you drive. We take stands in different locations in the same woods we are driving. Then the deer never know where to expect us.''

Spence also will change the direction he drives. He may drive a particular woodlot from north to south two or three times. But on the third or fourth time, he may drive that same woodlot from south to north or from east to west to keep the deer from patterning the drivers. Although most man-drives cover several acres, the Spences also will make a drive through a briar patch that only may be 30 yards wide by 50 yards long.

Have a Two-Man Drive

Often Donald and Jody Spence hunt with their family and friends and may have four to six standers, although Donald Spence prefers not to have more than four standers. When Spence hunts with a large group like this, he often will have two people driving deer.

The first driver walks 75 to 100 yards ahead of the second driver. His job is to let the deer know a hunter is in the woods. The first driver will spook some bucks toward the standers. The second driver moves as quietly as possible. Oftentimes deer will circle the first driver to attempt to slip out behind the first driver. Then the second driver will be in a position to take this buck.

The Spences' silent driving technique produces large numbers of bucks for them and their family and friends each season using a variety of weapons. Donald Spence has learned how to get inside the mind of a trophy whitetail and not only determine where the deer will go but why and how fast the deer will move. Spence prides himself not only on his ability to move deer to standers but also on his skill to move the deer slowly enough so that he or his hunters will get a shot.

Using Donald Spence's silent driving tactics, you and your hunting buddies can be far more effective, put on more man-drives each day you hunt and bag more and bigger bucks.

CHAPTER 7

DOUBLE CALL TO BAG
BIG BUCKS

Finally the 9-point buck we had watched for some time moved away from the herd of other bucks and does. He had heard the rattling of antlers produced by Steve Warner, wildlife biologist and vice-president of Bushlan Camouflage Company, and the grunt calls of Rod Haydel, president of Haydel's Game Calls.

"We've got him hooked now. All we have to do is reel him in," Warner said as he continued to lightly click the large antlers together.

When the rattling stopped, Haydel gave short calls on his grunt tube. The buck listened and continued to circle to our right.

"The buck will circle downwind of us before he comes in," Warner said. "Get ready John! When you have an open shot, prepare to make it. The next time Rod grunts and the buck stops, make the shot."

I had come to Texas to learn a new technique for calling deer, commonly called double-calling. This tactic could involve two or three hunters.

From what I saw and learned, I believe double-calling deer is much more effective than if a single person tries to call deer alone. With this tactic, I believe two or three hunters can see and take twice as many bucks in a day of hunting as one hunter can.

In the early days of professional football one athlete might play both offense and defense and be required to play several different positions on both the offensive and defensive teams. However, as the game developed, teams soon learned that having specialized players at each position on both offense and defense helped them perform more effectively, score more touchdowns on offense and stop more touchdowns being scored on defense than if one man tried to play two or three positions. From what I saw of double-calling, this philosophy also could be incorporated successfully in to deer hunting.

The buck was in the clear now. The crosshairs of my Simmons Whitetail scope were on the buck's shoulder. When I heard Haydel grunt, I saw the deer's ears go up. The animal froze like a statue. Gently I squeezed the trigger until the rifle reported. But instead of the buck's piling up in a heap as I expected, he began to trot up the hill. I was dumbfounded. I knew I had shot accurately and that the shot I delivered should have put the buck down instantly. But the animal still walked off as though he never had been hit.

"Take the second shot," Warner instructed.

At that moment Haydel grunted. The buck stopped again, and I fired a second time. This time I aimed square in the middle of the deer's back as he went away from me and up the mountain. The second shot, unlike the first, dropped the buck in his tracks. I still was puzzled, however, about why I had missed the first shot. My aim was steady. I'd squeezed the trigger, not jerked it. The shot felt right. But the buck didn't go down. At first I wanted to blame the rifle or the scope. However, then I remembered I had just sighted the rifle in two days before and I had taken all precautions to make sure my scope wasn't bumped.

When I got close to the buck, I saw that my rifle nor the scope was to blame. The surprising good news was that neither was I. Although the bullet had landed exactly where I had aimed, apparently the 7mm Magnum had gone through the deer so quickly the energy from the bullet had not caused the damage at that close range I had hoped it would. But I was proud of my trophy-racked buck, the hunt we had made, and the opportunity I had had to learn how, where, when and why double-calling bucks is so effective.

The more you can do to simulate a trophy buck fight, the more likely you'll be to call up a buck like this -- (Drawing by Jim Tostrud).

Duet Calling

"I believe two hunters can call and take bucks more effectively than one hunter can," Steve Warner said. "As you saw this morning, the buck came in upwind of us. But when he had come a certain distance, he began to circle downwind, possibly in hopes of picking up our scent before he came in to investigate.

"Many times deer will come in from behind you when you call. Even if you hunt a thick bedding area and expect the buck to come straight out to you, you don't know for sure that buck is in that bedding region. Nor do you know he will come straight in when he hears the horns and the grunting. I'm convinced a better tactic is for the person with the grunt tube to sit facing one direction and call and the person with the rattling antlers to face the other direction and call."

The first apparent problem with this technique is that the person with the grunt call faces the opposite direction from the person using the rattling antlers. Then the sound of the rattling antlers will appear to come from one direction while the sound of the grunt call will come from another direction.

However, the person using the grunt call either can cup his hand over the barrel of the call so that the sound from the grunt call is thrown to the area where the rattling is coming from, or he can call to the side, which may give the impression of another buck standing off to the side of the battle and grunting while he watches the fight taking place.

One of the most effective ways to double-call bucks is when the hunter who is working the antlers stops his rattling sequence. The other hunter starts using the grunt call and points the call in the same direction that the rattling antlers have been heard. Then he begins to move the call as he grunts around the tree. This tactic will simulate a buck's walking away from the fight as bucks often do after they clash antlers. The buck may walk away five to 10 yards, turn around and come back to the first buck to continue to duel. The main advantage of having the two hunters facing opposite directions is that both hunters now have eyes at the back of their heads to look for deer that may approach from behind.

"One of the forms of rattling that has proved to be the most effective for me has been limb breaking," Warner mentioned. "I take one of the antlers, rake it down the side of the limb like a buck that is battling a bush and grunt at the same time. I've learned that sometimes I can call in

Rattling antlers will call in a buck, but they seem to work more effectively when used in combination with a grunt call.

bucks more effectively than when I clash the antlers together. Many times in the pre-rut, the rut and the post-rut, bucks will come in to investigate the sounds of another buck's raking his antlers against a bush or tree. Bucks have a natural curiosity that often requires them to visually identify other deer they hear in their area.

Trio Trophy Buck Calling

When three hunters go into the woods to take one buck, some sportsmen may feel this is an overkill. However, consider the deer drive when several hunters attempt to move deer into an area where one of many standers can get a shot. The number of hunters required to triple-call bucks is not nearly as important as the fact that this strategy is deadly effective. In one day of hunting in good deer country, all three outdoorsmen may bag bucks. Let's look at the responsibility each hunter has when they triple-call bucks.

The Shooter

This sportsman's sole responsibility is to see the buck, look for a clearing in the woods where he can take the buck, prepare for the shot and when the buck steps into an opening, deliver the bullet. This hunter can focus all his attention on making the accurate shot.

The Rattler

The sportsman responsible for rattling in the buck with rattling antlers must get the buck's attention and cause him to start moving toward the stand where the three hunters sit. Rattling antlers can be heard at much greater distances than the grunt call can. The antlers provide a long-range calling implement the hunter can use to make contact with the buck that often may be 1/4 to 1/2 mile away. Since most bucks will come to a fight, rattling antlers can be especially effective during the breeding season. However, as most hunters have learned, bucks often will clash antlers from the time they come out of the velvet and begin to spar until the end of the breeding when they shed their antlers. Therefore, rattling antlers can be used to lure in deer from long range throughout the length of deer season in most states.

The Grunter

The grunt tube produces an effective call to lure in bucks that may be 100 yards or less from the caller. As most sportsmen know, you can use the grunt call to say many different things to a buck. When used in conjunction with the rattling antlers, the grunt call simulates a buck fight much better than only using the antlers. As deer fight, they often grunt. Also in between the actual clashing of antlers, deer may grunt either as a sign of aggression or a sigh of relief after the battle is over.

To date I don't believe any wildlife scientist has conclusively determined why deer grunt or what they say when they grunt. But most biologists agree that the sound of deer grunting often will call in bucks.

Another unique advantage the grunter brings to the trio of callers is that if a buck begins to walk away before the shooter can take the shot, the grunter often will stop the buck's retreat. If the buck walks away from the sound of the rattling antlers, many times grunting can pull him back in to the shooter. If the buck is too close to rattle because he may spot the movement of the antlers and the hunter, then the grunt call solves this problem too.

By combining grunting and rattling, the sportsmen offer a double-barreled approach to deer calling. With two callers working together to maneuver the deer into position for the shooter, the chances of getting a good, clean shot are much better.

"Other than all these reasons I believe that three people can have more fun deer hunting than either one or two can," Haydel said.

While one hunter rattles antlers, the author, pictured here, blows on a grunt call.

"Determining calling techniques, where to set up, when to call, when to shoot and enjoying the thrill of a successful hunt can be much more fun if you have two buddies, and you all share the experience. Besides when you go three-on-one for a buck, you also have two more backs and double the number of arms and legs to help drag the deer back to your vehicle."

Solo Double-Calling

I believe calling bucks with one or more friends is much more entertaining and effective than solo-calling deer. However, if you hunt alone, you can double the effectiveness of your calling by combining rattling antlers with grunt calls when you attempt to lure in deer.

No form of hunting aid always will produce a buck on any given day. But on some days, certain types of calls can and will be more effective than other calls. For instance, on one day you may not be able to get any deer to come to the sound of rattling antlers. However, you may have bucks run all over you if you begin to use the grunt call.

Instead of being an either/or deer caller, why not use both calls and double your effectiveness? I believe the best way to view the power of rattling antlers and grunt calls is to consider the rattling antlers as your long-distance call and the grunt call as your close-quarters call. Of course there also are sound arguments for why rattling antlers can be used as a close-in call and the grunt tube can be utilized as a long-distance call. For instance, by only tinkling the antler tips together or barely raking a bush with antlers, you can give a soft, subtle call that will bring a deer in from 50 yards or less. By using a magnum grunt caller on a windy day with the wind at your back, you also may grunt up a buck 1/4-mile away.

However, the sound of rattling antlers generally can be heard at a much greater distance than a grunt tube can. I also believe that the sharp crack of the antlers may get the buck's attention faster than a muffled grunt call will. But when a buck is in close and can see those antlers moving when you rattle them, he also may spot you.

Too, if he's a buck that has just been in a fight, he may not want to come closer for fear of getting in another altercation. However, if he hears a soft, grunting sound, he may think the battle is over, and the combat has waned to the point that the deer engaged in the fight pose no threat to him. Then he will come on in to where the hunter can see him. By using the grunt call when the buck is in close, you also can give the call without having to move your arms or hands. By reducing the amount of movement that the deer can see, you drastically increase your odds for taking that buck instead of spooking him.

Deer calling is an evolving process of bringing deer to the hunter. Each year we learn more and better strategies for calling big bucks more effectively. However, as we loaded my 9 point up and headed back to camp, I was more convinced than ever that using two calls and possibly two hunters was a much more effective way to lure in a trophy deer than only relying on one type of call.

CHAPTER 8

TRACK TROPHY BUCKS
IN THE SNOW

Norman LeBrun must have known these winding Canadian woods roads as well as his mother's face. At least I hoped he did. He was speeding his old green pickup over the freshly fallen snow like Dale Earnhardt banking into the pits at Darlington.

But as we reached our hunting area, his mood changed. He slowed down the truck and focused on the edge of the road. The conditions were ideal for tracking. Before long the truck came to a halt. LeBrun walked to the front of the truck and hunkered down toward the snow. We had cut a set of deer tracks.

Canadian Tactics

"That's a buck track, and he's moving slowly," LeBrun said, his pleasant accent revealing his French-Canadian roots. "We can catch him in 15 minutes or so."

"Say what?" I thought to myself LeBrun must have assumed I was a novice. Everyone knew you couldn't tell the sex of a deer by looking at its track, and you certainly couldn't tell how far away it was. I decided LeBrun was just trying to give me an anecdote for my story. Being the good reporter, I played along.

"So, Norman, exactly how can you tell so much from that track?" I asked, carefully adding a bit of skepticism, perhaps even sarcasm, to my voice.

But LeBrun was all business as he answered, "See how the deer drags his toes as he lifts his foot to walk? Bucks make this kind of track, not does. Usually when you see a track with the back toes dragging, the deer will be a buck.

"We can be sure the deer went across the road after the snow stopped falling, and he can't be more than 15 minutes in front of us if he keeps going at the same pace. But if we stand here and continue to talk, we may not catch up to that buck until next week. If you want to kill a buck, get your gun, and let's go."

I loaded my .243 and checked my riflescope to be sure it was clear of snow. LeBrun had begun to move away from the road and into the evergreens. I looked at my watch and saw the time was 2:15 p.m.

LeBrun, moving deliberately, stalked quickly through the snow, hardly looking at the track as he kept pace. Then he froze.

"There he is," LeBrun whispered.

The buck stood about 50 yards away in the trees, quartering ahead slightly and looking in the other direction. Before I brought my rifle to my shoulder, I turned my wrist and saw the time was 2:33 p.m. I brought the scope up and could tell the buck was at least an 8 pointer, perhaps a 9 pointer. I slowly brought the crosshairs just behind the animal's shoulder and squeezed the trigger. The deer bolted only a few yards before piling up in the snow.

"I thought you said we only needed 15 minutes to catch up to the deer," I quipped, offering a kidding compliment. "By my watch, 18 minutes passed before we reached the deer."

LeBrun looked up with a big smile as he bent over the downed animal. "If you hadn't wasted so much time asking me so many questions and getting your gear out of the truck, we would have caught up to this deer in 10 minutes!"

I laughed. I learned never to try to outsmart the veteran guide of Anticosti Island. LeBrun was intimately familiar with Anticosti, a large patch of land rising above the Gulf of St. Lawrence in eastern Quebec, Canada. The island has become famous for its whitetail hunting and two- deer limit. We dressed and dragged the deer back to the truck and loaded it. We still had several hours of daylight left, and LeBrun suggested we find another buck.

These two bucks were taken by the author by snow tracking on Anticosti Island.

An hour or so later we came across a place where four deer had walked across a clearing in the spruce forest. As LeBrun studied the tracks, he looked up at me and asked, "This one is a buck track. Can you tell?"

The dragging hoof mark was obvious among the three doe tracks. I nodded and smiled, and the hunt was on. An hour later we caught up to a nice 6 pointer. Once again, when my rifle reported, the buck fell in the snow. This time, LeBrun had misjudged the time required to kill the deer by only 10 minutes. Since LeBrun knew I was keeping track, his excuse this time came voluntarily.

"The snow was deep," LeBrun said. "But I thought you would be able to move through it quicker than you did."

We dragged the deer out of the dark forest and loaded it in the pickup next to the first. Then we took another wild ride down the snowy back roads.

Back home in Alabama, I never had the opportunity to do much snow tracking. The premise of finding and sneaking up on a mature whitetail buck seemed unlikely. But in hindsight, the skills involved in tracking were logical. LeBrun was a master; his precision in interpreting the tracks was obviously honed by vast experience.

"I've hunted deer all my life and guided hunters on Anticosti for 20 years," LeBrun said. "I work seven days a week for three months guiding hunters and trying to find deer. The little things -- the details I find in the snow -- help me determine the size and sex of the deer and how fast we can catch up with it."

LeBrun also uses the forest and weather conditions to fullest advantage.

"One reason I could tell how quickly we could get to the deer was because there was some wind today," he said. "The wind caused the trees to rattle their branches, knocking the snow off. All that rattling and even the thud of the snow covered the sound of our footsteps. Because everything else in the woods moved, I didn't think the deer would be spooked even if they saw us. I knew we could move swiftly to the bucks and get them in a hurry -- if you could shoot straight."

Tracking deer is not a technique for the impatient nor for the hunter who only spends three or four days a season in the woods. Recognizing the subtle clues and developing the almost sixth sense good trackers possess comes from lifetimes in the woods.

Northeastern Tracking Techniques

Perhaps the best-known tracker in the United States is 68-year-old Larry Benoit of Waterbury, Vermont. He and his sons have taken dozens of 200-pound-plus bucks in the northern New England mountains -- all by tracking -- and the family has been the subject of numerous articles. A fifth-generation Iroquois, Benoit has tracked deer for 59 years, first learning the skill from his father.

"A small deer track does not always mean the buck is a little deer," Benoit said. "Some bucks have smaller feet than others. But for a novice tracker, finding a big track is the best way to start looking for a large buck.

"To tell if you're tracking a buck or a doe, look for the little holes antlers make in the snow when the deer bends over to feed on a slope or a bank. Or, notice scrapes on trees where a buck has left signs as he feeds. Does leave a puddle when they urinate. Bucks leave a puddle and drops leading away from the puddle."

Moving slowly and looking ahead of the track, you often will see your buck of a lifetime.

Determining the size of a buck is more difficult. Although Benoit looks for many different signs, the main clue is the depth of impression left by the buck's hoof. If a track sinks through the snow and deep into the ground (soil under the snow is often soft because it is insulated), and if the hoofs are splayed, you're on the trail of a bruiser. Also notice the gait of the track. Does and smaller bucks often have hoof prints running along a straight line. But the big bucks have wide shoulders and heavy haunches. A trophy buck will have prints that are staggered side to side.

Once Benoit locates a buck track, one that he knows was left by a deer weighing more than 200 pounds, he remains on the trail like a bloodhound. He has trailed big bucks for days at a time, bivouacking

Although snow tracking is a sport for loners, if you take up the challenge, you'll often find that trophy buck of a lifetime.

along the way or returning each morning to resume the chase, before killing them.

One of Benoit's most fascinating and potent traits as a tracker is his kinship with the forest. Benoit's recollection for details in the woods has become second nature. He pays close attention to weather and remembers all the buck tracks he comes across.

"You can tell how fresh the trail is by how soon you see the track after a snow, or if you walk through a region, see no tracks and return to that area within the day and a track is there," Benoit explained. "Pay attention and you can assess how much time has passed since the buck's walked through that area."

To tell how fast a buck is moving, Benoit analyzes a track's length of stride. If the tracks are relatively close together and lead in a straight line, Benoit knows the deer is walking. Tracks close together but meandering mean the deer is feeding. If tracks are at wide intervals, Benoit knows the deer is running or getting nervous. Benoit says that even if he jumps a deer, he keeps after it.

When he was younger and more nimble, Benoit would break into an all-out run to keep up with the deer. As long as the tracks indicated the deer was running, Benoit was unconcerned about making noise. He was more anxious about keeping up. He said bucks usually would not run very far before feeding or walking again.

When Benoit thinks the buck is slowing down, he also slows his pace and begins searching ahead for the buck. Totally focused and moving only his legs, he expects to see the deer. Benoit puts his toe down first and then brings the rest of his foot down on the snow to move as silently as he can. He says that he often finds the buck less than 10 minutes after he determines the buck has slowed down.

As a younger man, Benoit once trailed the same deer for 13 days, coming back to camp at night to eat, sleep and prepare for the next day's stalk. The buck had a distinctive track and traveled 14 to 20 miles a day, roughly in a circular pattern. Benoit saw the deer three times. When the deer spotted Benoit, it would run, walk with fast strides and then slow down to a normal gait.

As Benoit recalled, "The buck knew I was there. When he saw me, he'd move out quickly. But I don't believe bucks usually remember incidences for a long time. I think even if they spot you when you're

Big bucks often will move slowly through heavy snow.

tracking them, if you remain on the trail, they often may forget you're there.

"That's what I think happened with this buck. Finally I was able to get within 50 yards of him. He thought he was well-hidden because he was backed up against the side of a mountain holding in some thick spruce. But I moved silently and bagged him.

"Most hunters can't track bucks and bag them because they don't take the time to read the signs to see what the deer are doing and where they're going. They move too quickly. Walking slowly, being patient and reading every sign the deer leaves is the key to tracking big bucks."

Woodsmanship is yet another key to successful tracking. Benoit intimately knows the woods in northeastern Vermont and the areas of Maine where he hunts. Most hunters only will travel 200 to 300 yards from a road to hunt. Benoit usually begins his stalk two to three miles away from roads and other hunters. Big bucks are rarely found in areas that receive heavy hunting pressure.

To be able to stay on a track, Benoit carries a form of trail mix, a high-energy food, to help him continue his stalk without having to break

Heavy snow will slow down the large bucks -- (Drawing by Kelli Breland).

Because very few people hunt in deep snow, you'll often find big ones.

for lunch -- or even dinner in some circumstances. He dresses lightly, wearing Duofold long underwear, wool pants, a light-cotton shirt, a flannel shirt over the cotton and a woolen coat over the flannel. Dressing in layers , Benoit can track all day without becoming too hot or too cold.

Midwestern Trailing Strategies

Noble Carlson of Hobolith, Minnesota, is another of the country's best deer trackers. But nearly every season, Carlson bags the kind of bucks most hunters wish to take once in their lifetime. A humble man, Carlson cannot escape the fame of his accomplishments. Tracking down and killing 200- pound-plus whitetails year after year is news that gets around.

When Carlson begins his hunt, he looks for a round and wide track rather than a sharp and pointed one. Since few deer live in the Lake

Superior area where he hunts, the bucks must advertise often for does by making scrapes. Because of rocky terrain, the bucks wear down their hooves and leave rounded tracks. In contrast, the track of a doe or young buck often will be no more than a tiny V with the rear portion of the hoof leaving a light imprint or none at all.

As Carlson follows a track, he reads it like a how-to book. Each step of the way, the buck's track tells Carlson what the buck is doing. A buck walking in the snow will leave drag marks and double imprints -- the dewclaw making the second mark. If the buck is running, or if it is very heavy, the hooves will splay under the pressure. A galloping buck leaves imprints at about six-foot intervals.

If the buck is moving in a straight line and the tracks are wide, Carlson knows the buck is trotting and going cross- country. In that event, Carlson moves as fast as he can to try to stay up with the deer. He doesn't worry about making noise when he's moving quickly. By watching the track, he can predict the deer's movements. He also wears felt-pack inserts inside galoshes that zip up the sides. This footwear combination seals out the cold and the moisture yet is very soft. The pliable soles of the galoshes allow Carlson to feel the ground under his feet. Then he can move before breaking a twig or branch.

If Carlson sees that the track starts a meandering pattern, he slows down his stalk. He has learned that when a buck begins to wander through the woods, it is looking to bed. He also watches the track for signs of the buck making a large circle. Mature bucks often will circle and look back over their tracks to see if they're being pursued.

When Carlson sees the track begin to circle, he attempts to get downwind of the buck and position himself on the side of a mountain. Getting above the action on the hillside, Carlson can spot the buck when it circles back. He usually takes a stand one-third of the way down the mountain. Carlson says that 90 percent of the deer he takes are shot when the deer make circles to look back over their trails. Most of the deer he takes weigh more than 200 pounds.

Norman LeBrun, Larry Benoit and Noble Carlson became expert whitetail trackers by first becoming students of the forest. Each day in the woods, they learn more about the ways of the whitetail. Each man has a singleness of purpose in his hunting pursuit. But all three agree the best way to become a proficient tracker is to study deer-movement patterns in the snow and spend enough hours in the woods to learn what the tracks are saying. Those who pay close attention will learn that these tracks often speak volumes about trophy bucks.

CHAPTER 9

HUNT CATTLE COUNTRY FOR MONSTER-SIZED BUCKS

Trophy bucks often live in cattle country and can be taken by those who know how to hunt them. Although in the past open spaces, cattle on a distant hill, and cowboys mending fences and driving cattle have been our perceptions of cattle country, today's picture often is that of a rancher in a pickup or a cowboy astride an all-terrain vehicle.

Because of the wide-open spaces, most deer hunters do not think of cattle country as deer country. But Ed McMillan of Brewton, Alabama, has grown up in cattle country and has hunted the white-tailed deer there most of his life.

"Some of the biggest bucks in any region often will be found in cattle country, for several reasons," McMillan explained. "All the ingredients present in cattle country that put weight and antlers on cattle also put weight on deer, including an abundance of food, fertilized pastures and little or no harassment, especially in the cattle country of the East and Midwest."

However, when most hunters see big pastures and few woods, they automatically dismiss the possibility of whitetails being present in these places. Few hunters realize that large, mature bucks have regular routes through these wide-open spaces.

"Just at daylight, big bucks will move from small heads of woods across pastures to thickets and bedding areas," McMillan said. "Deer like to cross in the middle of pastures, where they have a lot of open space around them. The bucks feel secure in crossing these pastures because they are rarely if ever shot at on these routes. Year after year, deer will travel the same trails through the middles of pastures they historically have used.

"I believe deer must learn at an early age the traditional routes of travel they can take between and through pastures. Most landowners will tell you where these routes are and what time of day they usually see deer crossing these open pastures. Once you find a good crossing in the middle of a pasture, you can hunt that same crossing year after year and consistently take bucks. I have found the most productive time to hunt these open areas is during the rut, when the biggest bucks travel the most, chasing the does."

Why Hunt Fence Lines

According to McMillan, "When you hunt fence lines, learn where the deer are crossing them, since deer often have one particular place in the fence where they will cross. You may be able to see the trail where the deer are crossing or telltale signs in the wire. For instance, if the deer jump the fence, they'll often leave white hair from their stomachs on the top strand of the wire. If the deer are going under the fence, you may see short brown hair from the deer's back, indicating it has crawled under the fence. Usually you'll find some type of deer hair at the point where the deer cross the fence.

"Your best chances for bagging a trophy buck probably will be when you locate a spot where the deer go under the fence. From my observations, I've learned even bucks with large racks may prefer to go under a fence rather than over it. By taking a stand 50 to 75 yards downwind of a fence crossing, you may get a shot at a buck when he stops and starts to go under the fence or stands up on the other side."

How to Hunt Small Patches of Cover

Three techniques pay dividends for hunting small cover in cattle country. Although deer will cross open pastures throughout the year, prior to the rut they often will hold in small woodlots where they can find acorns, browse and be protected by cover. Other spots where deer often stay during daylight hours in cattle country will be in weeds beside ditches, thick cover on a small hill or any patch of cover in the middle

Because cattle country is often very open with few, thick-cover places for a buck to hide, most hunters never look in those places for big bucks.

of an open field. The bucks will remain in these places during daylight hours because they can see danger approaching from any direction.

Stand Hunting

"To hunt thick cover in cattle country, you must identify the areas where the deer bed down at daylight, know how to reach these spots with a favorable wind before daybreak and take a stand," McMillan reported. "If you don't go into your stand under the cover of darkness, you will spook the buck you are trying to take."

Man-Drives

When you hunt small woods with open pasture on either side, you often can drive the deer out of the woodlots and into the openings where you can get a shot. However, to be successful, you must know which trail the deer will take out of the thick cover to cross the pasture, and then you must drive that woodlot more than once.

"This past season, my brother and I hunted a finger of woods about a mile long and 500 to 800 yards wide that divided two pastures," McMillan recalled. "I put my brother on an escape trail I knew the deer were using on one side of the head of the woods. Then I walked up the other edge of the woods, leaving a scent trail to create an invisible barrier to ensure the deer would not leave the woods that way.''

McMillan has found that blocking one side of a small woodlot with human odor to fence the deer in and make them move in the direction of the stander is a productive means of hunting small heads of woods in cattle country.

Once McMillan laid down this scent trail, he went to the end of the woodlot and began to move slowly through the timber.

''I could see deer getting up in front of me, but the deer didn't want to leave the woods to cross the pasture,'' McMillan explained. ''I walked a zigzag pattern to attempt to force the deer out of the woods so my brother could get a shot. Although I saw plenty of does, I never spotted a buck. No deer came out of the woods on my first drive.''

McMillan is convinced the key to driving deer is to walk slowly and quietly through the woods and not spook the animals. Unlike some hunters, McMillan's objective is to make the deer sneak out of the woods to avoid him. Then the stander will get a walking shot instead of a running shot.

''After the first trip through the woodlot, I walked back up the same side of the woods where I'd laid my scent trail the first time,'' McMillan continued. ''Although I hadn't seen any bucks, I thought at least one buck should have been in that area and maybe he just hadn't gotten up.''

Often, McMillan will drive the same woods two or three times before the bucks leave the woodlot and walk out into the pasture. In thick-cover areas surrounded by open pastures, deer may get up and run 50 to 100 yards, move off to the side of or out of the way of the driver, lie back down and let the driver pass by them. Deer quickly learn this behavior after a particular woodlot has been driven once or twice by hunters.

McMillan had seen 10 to 15 does and yearlings on his first drive. But on his second drive, five bucks got up and moved toward the pasture.

''Because the woods were relatively clean, I was surprised I hadn't spotted those five bucks on my first drive,'' McMillan said. ''However, on my second drive, I had put out enough human odor and the deer had

Often if you move to a thick-cover hideout in cattle country, you'll catch a big buck coming back to his bedding area just at daylight.

seen me enough that they had to get out of the woods and move across the pasture.''

When the deer finally slipped out of the woodlot and started across the open pasture, McMillan's brother bagged a nice 6 pointer that weighed 180 pounds. He let the four other bucks continue across the field.

''One of the reasons more hunters don't bag big bucks when they put on drives in small woodlots is because they assume they've moved all the deer out of the woods when they've gone though those woods one time,'' McMillan observed. ''I'll often move through the same head of woods two and even three times to make sure I've put enough pressure on a buck -- if there's one in that area -- and left enough human odor for him to smell to force him to leave the woods and cross the pasture."

Stalk Hunting

The drive tactic will produce bucks in woodlots on cattle ranches, but when you hunt by yourself, you also can stalk these same regions. McMillan starts his stalk downwind or across the wind when he moves into these little heads of woods.

"I hunt one step at a time," McMillan said. "I move very slowly and stop about every 50 to 60 yards to sit still for about 15 minutes. Because cattle often move through these same woodlots, usually the underbrush will be trampled or eaten. Generally, the woodlots in cattle country are open. The slower you move and the longer you wait, the more likely you are to see deer.

"Because the woods are so open, your human odor will travel quickly through the woodlot, if you don't have a favorable wind for hunting, and spook deer," explained McMillan. "That's why I never hunt a small woodlot without the wind in my face or without a crosswind to carry my odor out the other side of the woodlot. If I hunt with a crosswind up one edge of the woods, my human odor travels across the woods and moves all the deer ahead of it. Therefore, if I move up one edge, enough odor goes across the woods to cause deer to get up and move in front of me all the way to the other edge of the woodlot."

How to Make the Shot on a Cattle-Country Buck

When you hunt in large pastures, you may have to make long shots.

"I like a .264 Winchester Model 70 Magnum because it shoots much flatter than a 7mm Magnum will," McMillan reported. "I use a Nikon 3-9X variable scope, since I want maximum brightness as well as accuracy. When you hunt early and late and must take a long shot, you need the brightness in the scope to help you pick out the target better. I also use Nikon or Swarovski binoculars to help me see the buck and his rack before I prepare for the shot."

McMillan chooses an unorthodox aiming point.

"I aim about two inches in front of the point of the shoulder, in the neck region, when I'm hunting a buck in a pasture, because most of the time the buck will be walking across a pasture," McMillan explained. "Aiming just in front of the point of the shoulder in the neck area means if the buck does take a step as I squeeze the trigger, the bullet still will

If you take a stand on an escape route a buck will have to use, many times you can get a shot at a buck running across an open field.

hit the lung area. Also, if I hit in that neck region, the deer usually will drop in his tracks rather than run off.''

Many times, McMillan will sit on a fence line and watch pastures. To make an accurate shot, he rests his rifle on the top or the side of the fence post. If he's hunting in the edge of the timber, he always uses a tree to steady his aim.

To bag a cattle-country buck, the hunter must sit still, especially when hunting in open pastures. Only move to take a shot when the trophy deer has his head down or is walking away from you.

How to Get Permission to Hunt

Often trophy bucks will be found in cattle country because many landowners, especially in the East and Midwest, do not permit hunting around their livestock. They are concerned that a white-faced cow may be mistaken for a white-tailed deer. Therefore, gaining access to these game-rich hunting lands can be difficult.

The lands McMillan hunts are his family's lands. When asked what may convince a rancher to let others hunt his cattle-country bucks, McMillan responded that, ''One of the most critical keys to gaining access to any land but most especially to cattle lands, is the degree of trust a hunter can develop with the landowner. Also, to gain access to cattle-country bucks, a hunter has to be able to offer a landowner some type of incentive that outweighs the risk of property damage. One of the best incentives I know is to offer to come onto the land after deer season and hunt coyotes.''

Coyotes, which have spread across much of the country, with particularly large populations in the South, pose a major problem for all livestock owners, especially cattlemen. During calving season, coyotes may kill young calves, which is a huge loss to stockmen. If you offer to come in after deer season and hunt the coyotes that pose a threat to the farmer's livestock, you can begin building a trust required for getting permission to hunt his deer during deer season.

''Once a rancher knows you'll put fences back up, help to protect his property, eliminate a problem like the coyotes for him and that he can trust you to do what you say you'll do, then he's more likely to grant you permission to hunt his deer during deer season,'' McMillan emphasized. ''That bond of trust is what opens locked gates and allows you to enter what has been or is posted property. Most hunters fail to realize the friendship and trust they develop with a landowner is not only the key ingredient to obtaining permission to hunting cattle country but also to continue to be able to hunt on these lands. You must let the farmer know that even during deer season, you are more concerned about his cattle than you are your hunting and that if you have the opportunity to take a buck and a coyote at the same time, you will choose to bag the coyote. Then, more than likely, you'll continue to have access to that property and often be able to hunt lands no other hunter can.''

Why Cattle-Country Bucks Are So Big

Because few hunters hunt in cattle country, in many areas the bucks survive long enough to grow to maturity, with heavy body weights and large antlers. But cattle- country bucks often will be the biggest bucks in a region because of other reasons.

"Most cattlemen graze their cattle in areas with the types of soil that produce plenty of nutrition to fatten their cattle," McMillan said. "These good soils also produce bigger and better deer."

To get maximum yield from their cattle, ranchers often fertilize their pastures to increase the amount of grass each pasture produces and to increase the quality and the food value of that grass. Too, the fertilizer on the pasture increases the food value for the deer. Also, cattle-country bucks often grow bigger and faster than deer in other regions because the nut trees around these pastures receive some of the benefits of the fertilizing. These trees yield more and sweeter nuts than nut trees in open woods.

The nut trees and other browse the deer eat also will have fewer animals feeding on them than in big-woods areas. Therefore, the food is more plentiful and the deer have more to eat.

Getting rid of the coyotes that feed on calves in the calving season also eliminates the predators that feed on fawns when the does drop their young. The landowner who protects his land from marauding packs of dogs and coyotes is also preventing the deer from being harassed by the same animals. Good cattle management results in highly productive deer management.

Another factor that may help cattle-country bucks grow to such enormous size is the mineral blocks set out for cattle, which are also used by deer. Many cattle farmers also grow row crops like corn and soybeans to feed to their cattle, and deer also will feed on these same crops before and after the harvest.

Why Hunters Overlook Cattle-Country Bucks

"Most hunters believe the deeper you go into the woods, the better your odds are for taking bigger bucks," McMillan commented. "But my family owns some large woodlots as well as cattle ranches. I consistently take more big bucks on the cattle ranches than I do in the woods. Large bucks often stay in little places in wide-open spaces where no one looks for them. Because most hunters believe small, thick-cover places in cattle country can't, don't or won't hold trophy bucks, the majority of hunters overlook these spots."

How to Hunt Cattle-Country Bucks

One of the differences you will find when you hunt cattle-country bucks is that you will hunt individual deer rather than going into the woods and hoping to see a group of bucks or any buck. To take a trophy-sized, cattle-country buck, you must find, pattern and hunt that individual deer. You have to develop strategies to see that deer in a place and at a time when you can take him.

Probably the most efficient way to scout for these bucks is to talk to the ranch hands on the property. Although the owner may be a good source of information, the ranch hand who works with the cattle every day will see and know the haunts or the whereabouts of just about every buck on the property. The ranch hand can tell you what time of day he spots the buck in open country, where he sees the buck traveling and often give you the best hunt plan for bagging that buck.

"Another excellent source of information that can lead you to a big cattle country buck is to talk to the rural letter carrier," McMillan said. "The mailman's out on the road every morning before and at first light. The mailman will see these big bucks crossing pastures and roads throughout the county as he goes about his route. He may know where to find more big bucks than even ranch hands do."

Hunting cattle country in the East and the Midwest where few other hunters hunt will help you find some of the biggest bucks you ever will have the opportunity to take. By getting to know the landowner and helping him eliminate the coyotes on his land, you can develop a relationship that will provide some of the best trophy deer hunting available -- anywhere.

CHAPTER 10

USE YOUR TABLE-TOP TO BAG BIG BUCKS

You can find the buck you want to take this season or at least learn where he probably is while studying on your kitchen table. Most hunters spend too much time walking around in the woods and not enough time learning how to hunt their property and where bucks move. An aerial photo and a topographical map can show you where deer are most likely to appear, how to efficiently hunt your land and how to increase your hunting time and decrease your scouting time. Also aerial photos and topo maps can make dragging deer out much easier and allow you to get quickly to and from your stand.

Learning the Lay of the Land

Every piece of property is different with roads, creeks, rivers, drainage systems, thickets, open timber and a variety of land types. Because property lines most often do not form squares or rectangles, I first search for where the property lines are when I look at an aerial photo and a topo map. Most of the time, I'll take some type of marker and draw the property lines in on the aerial photo and topographical map.

Using a map allows you to shrink the amount of land you have to hunt. You also can designate with a marker road systems running through the property, which will permit quick and easy access into and out of the lands you want to hunt. Too, knowing where these roads are will keep you from getting lost and give you a way to orient yourself to

By using an aerial photo, you can find bottlenecks and funnels through which trophy bucks will move.

know exactly where the spot is you have chosen to hunt. You'll also see where the cliffs and the thick cover are as well as pinpoint the places where most hunters probably will hunt -- like big, open-wood areas. Studying an aerial photo can save you days of walking and driving and trying to learn the land.

"Once I determine what the land looks like from an aerial photo, the next landmarks I instinctively search for on the photo are the natural funnels on the property I hunt," Bo Pitman, lodge manager of White Oak Plantation in Tuskegee, Alabama, said. "I'm looking for places like a field that corners into a creek with a small hardwood strip between the two, a woods road that bends into a pine plantation and any other type of natural funnel where two kinds of terrain come close together and leave a small corridor through which deer can pass. These natural funnels are where I'll see the most deer movement and where the chances will be best for taking a deer on any piece of property."

Generally you will not find more than three, productive funnels on any 2000 acres of land. But you can see these funnels from an aerial photo and quickly will know where the best places are to hunt on that property. The bird's-eye view you get with an aerial photo gives you a much better, clearer picture of the land you want to hunt and even can tell you what types of trees you have on the property.

"Hardwoods will appear like little, round blobs on an aerial photo, whereas pine trees will look smoother like the brush strokes of a paint brush," Pitman explained. "You can tell by an aerial photo whether the area has both pine and hardwoods, all hardwoods or planted pines by the texture of the trees on the photo."

If you bowhunt and plan to hunt around nut trees, the aerial photo can show you where to find these nut trees. If you hunt pine thickets later in the season, because the deer hide in the pines to dodge hunter pressure, the aerial photo will tell you how to go to these sites.

Although aerial photos can give you plenty of information about the land you hunt if you learn to use them, aerial photos also can lie to you. Because aerial photos purchased from the U. S. Geological Survey only are made about once every 10 years, knowing how old a photo is can tell you how reliable the information is you see. Perhaps the land has been timbered, the fields have been allowed to grow up, agricultural practices have been implemented, or a tornado or a windstorm has blown down numbers of trees since the aerial photos was made. Then your aerial photo will not have the precision a recent photo will. Sometimes hunters charter a private plane and fly over their hunting leases making photographs before and after deer season to give them up-to-date maps to study and use for making their hunt plans. Although chartering a small plane to photograph your hunting lease seems a great expense, if you calculate the number of days you must spend walking around in the woods to obtain this same information, you'll see the cost is negligible.

In the West, an aerial photo is not as critical to success as it is in the East. The West has little timber in places and more mountains and valleys, which means a topo map may be a better hunting tool for finding deer.

But a topo map also is very useful when hunting deer in the East in heavily timbered terrain. Although you may be able to tell the timber types and the general lay of the land from an aerial photo, you may not be able to see how the drainage system in the area creates bottoms and land relief. However, a topo map will give you that information.

Utilizing both aerial photos and topo maps will enable you to scout much quicker and more effectively.

The photos and maps you use to hunt your property are much like your ticket to a football game. The information on the ticket tells you where the stadium is located, has a diagram on the back that shows you where the section gate is that you must use to enter the stadium and also denotes which section you are supposed to sit in but doesn't show you your specific seat. I have known hunters who have studied aerial photos and topo maps and have walked into a natural funnel, a hardwood bottom or the edge of a field and have bagged a buck without ever actually scouting the land on foot. But, these instances are rare.

Moving from the Table to the Woods

The best times to study your maps is before and during hunting season. The most productive way to scout is to walk in the woods with your maps as soon as hunting season closes.

"When you go into the woods after hunting season, you usually can see where other hunters have been hunting, spot the trails deer have been using and learn the land quicker when the leaves are off the trees than if you go into the woods before hunting season begins," Bo Pitman reported. "By entering the woods after hunting season, you often will find the places where the big bucks have hid all year long and know where to find them in the absence of hunting pressure."

The second best time to scout woods utilizing your maps and aerial photos is during the summer or two to three weeks before hunting season. Go in and look for trails to try and spot deer. See if deer have used the funnels you've found. Study the changes in the land, and search for trophy-sized bucks. No matter how much you learn from an aerial photo and a topo map, you still have to ground-check the assumptions made from your maps to be successful.

"Another factor to consider is the type of woodlots you have to hunt," Pitman advised. "In many areas of the North, deer may concentrate in numbers of small woodlots. But in the South, deer can walk anywhere they want to go in large woodlots. If you have small woodlots to hunt, then you're limited as to where you can put up your stands. But if you have large woodlots to hunt, you can change your stands often."

Oftentimes from your maps, you can see where a buck like this has to hold to survive.

Pitman believes a stand that has been hunted from three times is not as effective as it is the first time it is hunted.

"When I ground-check an area I've located on my map and see my assumptions are right and that the deer are where I've thought, I mark that stand site on my map," Pitman said.

"I assume that after I've hunted out of that stand three or four times that deer in that area probably will change their movement patterns.

"Then I return to my map, look for another way to come into that general region from a different direction and pick another stand site. Usually I'll have four or five different paths to get to various stands in the same section of woods where I've found deer to be traveling.

"To be consistently successful in bagging a buck on any given piece of property, you must surprise the deer. You have to be in a place where he's not expecting you at a time he doesn't anticipate seeing you there.

"When you find a region after or before the season where deer travel, don't just choose one stand site. You may not be able to hunt from that stand on a certain day because of wind direction. Instead of having the wind in your face, the wind may come from your back and blow your scent into that area. Any time you find a good spot to hunt on your map or while scouting, always look for several alternative stand sites and different directions from which to come into that same region. Then when you listen to the weather report in the morning, and the weatherman tells you which way the wind is blowing, you'll know which route to pick and which stand site to utilize to hunt deer in that section of the woods."

Pitman also suggests you mark multiple stand sites on your map as well as designate which way the wind must blow for you to effectively hunt each site. By having this information on your map each morning before you leave for the woods, you can select the very best stands on your map to hunt from that day. Keep a pocket reference with the stands numbered and the wind directions designated you need to hunt from each stand. Then if the wind changes during the day, you will know which stands to move to and to hunt from with a favorable wind.

Using the Map as a Reminder

Most of us like to believe we have extensive memories, but we do not. Memory fades each year. However, if you record on your map the date and place where you bag each buck, the chances of returning to that same spot on or about that same day another year and taking another buck are very good, particularly if you've bagged a dominant buck.

Deer are creatures of habit and have a pecking order. These two factors mean that certain things happen every year in a deer herd in about the same place at about the same time. If you hunt over a food site such as an acorn tree, more than likely that tree will drop its nuts at about the same time each year. Usually deer in that area will come to

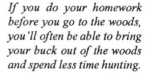

If you do your homework before you go to the woods, you'll often be able to bring your buck out of the woods and spend less time hunting.

that particular tree year after year. Therefore, a nut tree, a greenfield or any other type of food source where you have bagged a buck may produce a buck in coming years, if you can remember the exact spot. By marking that site on your map and recording the date, you will not have to rely on your memory.

If you discover a scrape line and take a buck along that scrape line, you may be able to hunt that same scraping region year after year. Often more than one buck will walk that specific scrape line. When the dominant buck, the animal that has made the scrape, is harvested, the next buck in the pecking order will become the dominant buck and probably use the same scrapes in the same places his predecessor has. By marking those scrape lines on the map and noting the date you take a buck off those scrape lines, you have a quick and easy reference to locate those scrape lines the next year and return to that same region at about the same time of year.

Hunting Bucks with Computers

Dr. Robert Sheppard of Carrollton, Alabama, belongs to several different hunting clubs and regularly hunts several leases each season.

"Each day I hunt, I enter the information from my hunt into a laptop computer," Dr. Sheppard reports. "I note how I get to each stand I hunt, the weather conditions, the number of deer I've seen by gender, where I take deer and what wind conditions I must have to return to hunt that same stand. I've been building this database for several years.

"Today when I get ready to hunt, I type in the name of the particular tract of land I want to hunt. I can find how to get to all my stand sites, determine what wind condition is favorable for hunting each of the stand sites and learn from which stand sites I've seen or taken bucks. I can cross-reference this information with the time of year I've hunted and select the stands where my chances are best for bagging a buck before I ever leave home."

Sheppard has proven that utilizing the power of the computer and recording all the information he can gather while hunting allows him to use the computer to process that information and choose the most productive stands to hunt from each day he is in the woods.

In the past, older hunters always have said you can't learn about deer hunting in any better way than actually putting in your time in the woods. However, today with the detailed maps available, the vast amount of information about deer known and the ability of the computer to process information about deer, outdoorsmen do not have to rely solely on their woods knowledge to be effective trophy deer hunters.

CHAPTER 11

ROAD HUNT TO TAKE TROPHY BUCKS

A brown muzzle eased out of the thick cover as a deer's eyes appeared. Finally a wide, high rack came into view. Cautiously, nervously, the buck took two steps into the road. A rifle reported. The buck stumbled and fell. The hunter had his trophy.

Automatically, when I hear the term, road hunting, I think of a poacher with a spotlight cruising up and down the highways, taking game illegally. However, a new system of road hunting has been developed that is legal and very effective, especially for taking large, monster-sized whitetails.

Selecting a Road

In most hunting areas, you will find woods roads, firebreaks, old logging roads, power lines or some other type of paths or clearcuts through the woods. Because these regions are so open, often hunters will not hunt them. However, one of the most effective ways to consistently bag whitetails is to learn to hunt these paths through the woods.

By driving these roads, firebreaks or trails at mid-morning, especially after an all-night rain has softened the ground, you can find tracks where deer cross the road during daylight hours. In snow country, you often can locate these road crossings much easier if snow has fallen. Also trails will be easy to see and well-defined. While hunting on Anticosti

Island in Quebec, Canada, our guide, Norman LeBrun, demonstrated that driving the roads after a major snowstorm was the most effective way to find where and when deer cross roads.

Once you have pinpointed where the deer are crossing, you will understand where to take a stand. When you know from which direction the deer go and come across the road, next you must determine what wind direction you must have to hunt that road crossing properly. Make sure on the day you plan to hunt that spot that the wind is blowing so it will carry your human odor away from the deer.

Generally on the days I scout roads, I will scout all the roads in the area I plan to hunt and make notes as to ...

* where the crossings are,
* which wind direction I need to have to hunt that road and
* where I can put my stand.

By taking a day to scout roads, power lines, trails and firebreaks, you will have productive road crossings to hunt all season long.

Hunting Roads Safely

"Because hunters often travel up and down woods roads and logging roads, I make sure no other hunter will come down the section of road I choose to hunt, that other hunters know exactly where I am and that I will be looking for game up and down that road," Larry Norton of Pennington, Alabama, a longtime avid hunter for deer who is a guide at Bent Creek Lodge in Jachin, Alabama, said. "Usually I paint the words, 'DANGER, HUNTER IN ROAD' on both sides of two cardboard boxes. I place the boxes on either end of the road I plan to hunt.

"Then any hunter traveling up or down the road will know exactly where I'm hunting, will not disturb me or the deer and will not walk into my hunt site. Generally if you stay off main roads, you rarely will experience hunter interference. However, I believe the signs are an added safety precaution to ensure better and safer hunting."

Choosing Stand Sites on a Road

A hunter can employ two effective types of stands -- a ground blind or a tree stand -- when hunting a road. By setting a portable ground blind up on the side of the road next to the cover, you can see up and down the road and have a greater ability to move around than if you sit in a tree stand. A ground blind also allows you to sit all day comfortably in one spot. However, ground blinds are solid masses of material and do not

If you'll look on the sides of roads, often you'll find good deer trails.

have the three-dimensional look of the woods. Often the wind will blow, and the whole side of a blind will move, which will spook deer. But leaning brush and limbs against the side of the blind will give the blind a three-dimensional look and make it less likely to spook deer.

I suggest setting up the blind the day before you plan to hunt. Then all you'll have to do is slide into the blind without ever making a sound. If you cannot put the blind up the day before the hunt, clear the spot where you will place the blind. Have the limbs and bushes readily available to lean up against your blind the next morning before daylight. Go to your stand site, set up the blind in the dark, and place the limbs against the blind. Be sitting in the blind while the woods are still dark.

Preparing a tree stand before your hunt is also important to your success. For a tree stand site to be the most effective, make as little noise as possible putting the stand up and going to or coming away from it. Having a ground blind or a tree stand pre-set the day before you want to hunt will minimize the amount of noise you make on hunt day.

Using a Drag

One of the problems associated with hunting roads is deer generally cross a road quickly since they realize they are exposing themselves. Often the deer may move so fast you cannot get a shot, which is why many road hunters see deer but do not actually bag them.

"This problem was one I encountered when I first started road hunting deer," Norton explained. "I tried using a forked stick to set my rifle on to keep my rifle pointed down the road toward the deer crossing. To take a shot, all I had to do was put the rifle to my shoulder, pick up the deer in the scope and shoot because the rifle already was steadied and pointing in the direction where the deer probably would cross."

However, even using this tripod-type rifle rest, Norton had little success bagging bucks that leaped or ran across roads.

"Because I knew I had to stop the deer in the road, I put Tink's-69 deer lure on a cloth drag and then drug the scent across the crossing and toward my stand," Norton reported.

Utilizing this technique, Norton was able to stop deer, often in the middle of the road, where he could take a shot, and actually lure deer to him by pulling the scent-impregnated drag toward his stand.

The key to successfully using a scent drag and any type of deer lure is to be sure the deer smell the lure and not your human odor. If you walk down the road pulling a drag, you risk the chance of having your human odor, especially from your boots, left on the ground at the same places where you are trying to put the deer lure. If the buck smells human odor instead of or at the same time he detects the deer lure, more than likely he will retreat back into the brush and not cross the road.

To prevent spooking the deer, wear knee-high rubber boots or hip waders when you drag the deer lure down the road. With this method, you can leave the lure on the road without adding your human odor.

Pulling Bucks out of Thick Cover

Oftentimes a road or a firebreak will be the only path through a clearcut, a pine plantation or a big briar thicket. That road may provide a clear shot for from 20 to 60 yards. I've seen many places where I've known big bucks must be holding but have found no way of getting into that thick cover without spooking the deer.

One place where a buck often will cross a road is under a bridge. Larry Norton, pictured here, looks for deer trails in these kinds of areas.

However, Larry Norton says that, "I use scent rags to pull bucks out of heavy cover. I dip rags in Tink's-69 and tie the rags to trees on the opposite side of the road from the cover where I think a buck is. The wind carries the deer lure into the thicket.

"I go to the end of the thicket and set up my ground blind on the edge of the road. I sit my ground blind on the opposite side of the thicket from where I expect the buck to be. The ground blind hides me from the deer's sight. Also if I keep one side of the blind zipped up, the blind captures and holds my human odor to keep it from drifting into or along the edge of the thicket where the deer is." Norton has discovered deer will come to the edge of thicket and look across the road for the scent they smell. Then they will begin to crane their necks and cautiously slip out of the cover.

Norton often changes the scents he uses depending on the time of year. "If I hunt during the rut, instead of Tink's-69, I may put Dominant Buck Urine on dehydrated Tarsal Gland to make the buck think there's

111

an intruder buck in his territory. If a big buck is in that thick cover, often he'll come out of the cover stiff-legged with his ears laid back and the hair on the back of his neck standing up at attention, ready to fight.''

One mistake hunters often make when hunting roads is to leave their scent dispensers out after they have completed their hunting for the day -- one of the surest ways not to bag a buck the next time you hunt this same road. Deer lure is most effective when utilized to lure in a buck that never has smelled the lure before. If lure is left out overnight or at any time when a hunter is not hunting and a buck comes in and smells that lure and does not see what he has expected to see -- a doe -- then more than likely he will not be fooled by that same lure again.

If you hunt a road through thick cover, do not hunt this spot more than once a week. Each time you return to set up your ground blinds and hunt this road, utilize a different type of deer lure from the time before. You may lure a buck out of heavy cover to a new smell.

Hunting Right-of-ways

Often hunters hunt power lines, gas lines and other right-of-ways that go through woodlots and fields. In most states, these right-of-ways are legal to hunt, and the hunters can see for great distances. Some hunters assume the more area they can view, the greater their odds are for spotting a buck. However, to increase your odds for bagging a buck, hunt only small sections of right-of-ways.

The most productive strategy for right-of-ways is to walk both sides of an entire right-of-way and look for trails that come to the edge of the clearing. Often the best spot to hunt may be along a right-of-way where a creek, a draw or a ditch crosses the right-of-way and thick cover or a terrain break is present that the buck can use to cross the right-of-way without being seen or without exposing himself very much.

I use a tree stand to get above these thick-cover areas or terrain breaks. Then I can look down into them. Often the thick cover crossing a power line may have a small opening in it where you can see deer moving. If there is no opening, I will go into the middle of that thick cover and cut a shooting lane that cannot be seen from either side of the cover but that opens up a clear site in the middle of that cover. Then I can spot a deer from my tree stand.   Most hunters look for deer in the open places along right-of-ways. To take a trophy buck, search for the

By driving down the highway and seeing deer crossing the road, Norton knows where to begin his scouting for bucks.

thickest cover or the most dramatic terrain break along that right-of-way and take a stand there.

Man-Driving a Right-of-Way or a Road

Hunters often use roads, right-of-ways or trails as stand lines when they man-drive to hunt deer. However, here are several considerations before using one of these paths for a stand line.

* Determine which way the wind blows. If the standers are on the road and the wind blows their scent into the area from which the drivers will come, the deer are less likely to come to the road. If you stand the road, be sure the wind is coming from the same direction from which you expect the deer to approach. By using this tactic, the drivers can utilize their human odor to move the deer to the standers.

* Do not stand in the road. To man-drive an area and use standers on the roads most effectively, the standers should be in tree stands on opposite sides of the road from where the deer will come. Then the hunters can shoot up and down the road without endangering each other

because their bullets will be aimed toward the ground rather than up the road.

* Put standers high enough into the trees to not only be able to look up and down the roads but also to see into the woods or thickets just past the road. Generally the deer being driven will approach a road and stop from six feet to 10 yards from the road. Then the animals slowly will approach the road. Once they reach the road, they will run or jump quickly across the road, often not permitting time for a shot. The best opportunity for a stander to get a shot at a deer standing still or moving slowly is just before the deer reaches the road. A stander must be on the opposite side of the road from which the deer is coming and high enough in a tree to see the deer when it is within 10 to 20 yards of the road before it crosses the road. The road acts as a stop sign that will cause a deer to walk slowly or stop and present the shot to the hunter before the animal crosses the road.

* Make sure the drivers walk as slowly as possible. Then their human odor will move the deer instead of frightening the deer with their whooping, hollering and crashing through the brush. Be certain the drivers wear hunter orange on their heads, chests and backs to make them highly visible to the standers.

This tactic of man-driving roads is highly productive and will put big bucks in your rifle or shotgun sights.

Before you practice any of these road-hunting strategies, make sure you legally can hunt the roads, right-of-ways, power lines, trails or firebreaks in your region. Learn what restrictions and regulations govern the hunting of roads in your area, and abide by these laws. Effective road hunting can aid you in finding and taking trophy bucks many other hunters ride or walk past each season.

114

CHAPTER 12

HUNT WETLANDS FOR BIG BUCKS

One fall several years ago, two buddies and I waded a swamp late in the season. We already had passed a small dry spot where the top of a downed tree on the ground was above the water. I had walked 10 feet from that place when I noticed my buddy look back over his shoulder, take aim with his rifle and squeeze the trigger. I didn't understand why he had taken the shot until I saw a nice 8 point roll off a little mound and into the water. When we reached the buck, I asked my buddy how he had seen the deer.

"I noticed some movement on tiny patch of ground," he said. "As I looked closely, I spotted the deer's antlers. In my riflescope, I could see the buck watching you. Apparently he hadn't seen me or perhaps thought I would walk on past him. I guess the buck knew you were walking away from him and posed no threat to him. He never saw me when I raised my rifle."

As we dragged the buck through the water and back to camp, I thought about how many bucks I probably had walked by each time I went into a swampy area. A hunting friend once told me that since an older age-class buck easily could see or hear me in a swamp, then more than likely the deer wouldn't get out of his bed. However, if he no longer could see or hear me, he would become nervous and might come out of his bed to look for me.

When you walk through wetlands like flooded timber or swamps and you reach a thicket, stand near that thicket. Don't move or say a word. Often the buck you are looking for will stand up and search for you.

Flood-plain bucks are some of the biggest and wariest deer to be found anywhere in the nation and particularly in the South. When Thor heaves his thunderbolts through the sky striking the clouds, and the rains come down, the South is often inundated with water. Rivers and streams overflow their banks, and the ground that the water spills over is revitalized with rich soil. River-bottom hardwoods produce the nut crops on which deer feed. Briar patches and thickets provide both food and shelter for whitetails. The dense undergrowth of wetlands helps deer to vanish from the hunter, and the vast expanses of water provide an easy way for deer to avoid danger.

But how do you hunt bucks with their massive antlers and their heavy body weights in these wetlands? How can you consistently produce bucks from these flooded timber areas?

How to Adapt Your Hunting to Wetlands

In most sections of the South, the floods arrive during the rutting season. However, if traditional scrape lines are underwater, then the hunter's time is wasted if he tries to take a stand near these scrapes. Deer travel through and feed in the water; however, they prefer to spend most of their time on dry land, which means you must find these above-water refuges to successfully hunt wetlands. Although I take bucks primarily off ridges running through a swamp or flooded timber sites, I also have bagged large bucks on patches of ground that aren't more than 10 feet in circumference with water all around them. These isolated spots of dry ground may be where you discover the bigger bucks, especially if some type of cover is on that place.

Scrape Lines

"Hunting deer in a flood plain is different from hunting deer anywhere else," explained Braz Webb, a hunting friend of mine from Bay Minette, Alabama, near the Gulf Coast. Webb hunts in the Delta country of south Alabama where much of the hunting is in swamplands and flooded timber.

"John, all the tactics you recommended in your book, 'The Science of Deer Hunting,' will work in the swamps," Webb said. "But the

Oftentimes the hunter who dons his waders and crosses water will find the bigger bucks.

hunting is closer in a swamp situation. You can't see deer as far in the thick cover of these river bottom swamps where we hunt as you can in the hills and hollows in other parts of the South.''

According to Webb, if you take a stand from 50 to 150 yards away from a scrape line not in a swamp and wait for a buck, you may get a shot. However, in swampy areas, you either must sit immediately on top of the scrape or no more than 30 yards away from the scrape to be able to see it and the trail leading to the scrape through the thick underbrush.

Logging Roads

In South Carolina where I hunt the Savannah River swamp at the Bostick Plantation near Estill, the only ways to hunt are to take a stand along logging roads that meander through the swamps or to stand near an old loading yard where logs once were stacked to be carried out of the swamp. These openings are the only places where you can see a deer at more than 30 yards.

A nice buck like this one often will hold in a swampy area where he can see and hear the hunter coming -- (Drawing by Jim Tostrud).

Because river-bottom swamps flood annually, they are so fertile and rich that vegetation grows up quickly. Thickets are much more numerous than in open woods. If you take a shot at a buck, you often must make a close shot. In many of these regions, you will hunt from permanent tree stands since only certain sites on the roads are out of the water.

Camouflage

One morning at first light on the Bostick Plantation, I was on a stand perched on a woods road. Before a doe started to cross the road, she stuck her head out and looked straight at me in my tree stand. Although I didn't move or breathe, I knew the animal saw me. She very slowly backed up and returned the same way she had approached the road.

Ten minutes later I had the same thing happen again. Although I was dressed in full camouflage, I believed the deer spotted the white of my face and hands.

I reached into my hunting coat and retrieved two tubes of grease paint. I put the black grease paint all over my face, neck and hands and streaked green paint on top of the black. The next deer that arrived at the edge of the road was a nice-sized 8 point. He looked in the tree stand and then peered across the road and began to walk across the road. The buck was about 20 yards from me when the crosshairs on my Browning Gold Medallion .243 found the point of his shoulder. I squeezed the trigger, and the fine buck went down.

The gun hunter must be totally camouflaged like the bowhunter because wetland hunting is close hunting.

Shooting Lanes

"When we hunt thick cover either in or along the edge of a swamp, we cut shooting lanes through the dense underbrush from our stand sites in three directions," said Hayward Simmons, the owner of Cedar Knoll Hunting Lodge in Allendale, South Carolina, also in the Savannah River swamp. "Most of the time when you see a buck in wetlands, he'll be crossing one of the outside shooting lanes, and you'll be unable to get a shot. However, you can aim at the next lane where you think the buck will cross. Then when he steps into that lane, you can take the shot.

"In swampy areas, big bucks stay in thick cover. Most of the time the cover they're in is so thick, you'll never be able to see them to take a shot. We've learned at our lodge that cutting shooting lanes through that thick cover will allow us to effectively harvest older age class bucks."

Wind

Another tactic I use in swampy flooded timber regions is to hunt deer with a stout wind blowing. If I can find an island or a long finger of woods jutting out into the water, I'll generally take a buddy or two with me to hunt this high ground. As the three of us approach the high ground, I'll move out in the water and wade to the far end of the island, being careful to keep the wind in my face. Then my human odor will be blown across the water and not onto high ground.

Once I reach the end of the island, I get out on the land and slowly and deliberately walk back and forth across the peninsula or the island. I'm careful to break sticks about every 10 to 20 yards, and I allow my human odor to blow down the island. Both tactics will alert the deer to my presence. As the deer smell and hear me coming, they often will begin to sneak out the other end of the island or peninsula where my friends are waiting to take their shots. This slow-stalking technique often will put walking bucks instead of running bucks in front of my friends' gunsights.

Recovery of Deer

A problem associated with hunting swamp bucks that Hayward Simmons has solved is how to recover deer once they're downed. Because deer can vanish quickly in this thick cover and often take to the water to escape, having a quality trailing dog is an absolute necessity. Cedar Knoll's Sunny is a yellow Labrador retriever that does not eat much, works long hours, does not complain, is excited about his job and has a fine nose.

"After the hunter takes a shot in our swamps, he does not come out of his tree stand to follow the deer," Simmons explained. "He is instructed to wait at his stand until I come to pick him up with the truck. Then the hunter doesn't leave any human odor in the woods, and he doesn't get lost in the swamp trying to find his deer. He also doesn't push the deer, which only may be wounded and just needs time to lie down.

"Once we pick up the hunters, we take them back to the lodge to eat either lunch or supper, depending on whether they're hunting in the morning or the afternoon. After the meal, several of us and Sunny will return to the stand where the hunter has shot. Even if the hunter thinks he's missed the deer, we still take Sunny with us to check out the hunt site."

I was with Simmons on three recoveries with Sunny. A 14-year-old boy had taken a shot at a buck in high grass. No blood was present at the spot where the boy had shot. The youngster wasn't sure whether he

Dragging a boat through the woods to paddle to an area other hunters can't hunt is a very aggravating process. However sportsmen who pay the price, often bag the bucks.

had hit the deer. However, in less than five minutes Sunny barked. We found the buck not 50 yards away in a thicket. The deer probably never would have been recovered without the dog.

The next morning, an older gentleman took a shot at a nice 8 point in an open acorn flat. Rain had fallen all morning long. The hunter was convinced the rain had washed the deer's scent away and Sunny wouldn't be able to locate the animal. When the yellow Lab was taken back to the stand site, he walked about 50 yards, barked and ran out through the swamp. Although the older hunter felt quite certain the deer had not run off in that direction, in 20 minutes, Sunny was sounding off like a beagle on a hot rabbit trail. When we reached the dog, the buck lay dead in the water.

The third and most impressive recovery Sunny made while I was at Cedar Knoll was at night. The hunter knew he had missed an 8 point. When Sunny went off barking on the trail, the man looked at me and said, "I know Hayward thinks a lot of that dog, but this time the dog is lying. He must have picked up a fresh track, because I know I missed that deer. I'm also sure the deer didn't run in that direction."

Fifteen minutes later, Simmons, who had been following Sunny, yelled out from the flooded timber, "Hey, come on down here. You've got a fine 8 point."

A writing friend of mine hunted the Bostick Plantation a couple of years ago when I did and bagged a 10-point buck the first day we hunted. On the second morning, the humidity was high, and a fog hung over the swamp. My friend hunted along a power line right-of-way that went through the swamp. In the mist, he spotted a deer he watched for at least 15 minutes.

When the deer stepped out of the fog, he could see him clearly with his Nikon Mountaineer binoculars. Although the buck was at about 100 yards, he could count 10 points on his rack. He lowered his binoculars and mounted his Remington .270. Resting his rifle on his tree stand railing, he took steady aim and fired. Immediately the buck vanished. Although he felt he had made a good shot, in the fog he couldn't tell whether he had hit the deer.

Perry Sauls of the Bostick Plantation came to pick him up later and brought his Labrador retriever with him. The dog searched the spot where my friend thought he had last seen the buck. But the Lab couldn't pick up the scent. Then after 10 minutes of searching, the dog went to the power line away from my friend's stand.

About 30 yards from where my friend thought the buck had entered the woods, the dog started to bark and move deep into the swamp. Sauls followed the dog on a dead run. The buck, which had lain down about 75 yards from the right-of-way, jumped when he spotted the dog and ran into the water with the dog right on his heels. When the buck hit the water, the dog grabbed the whitetail's neck, submerging the animal. The hunt was over.

Older age-class bucks may bed on the edge of water which they use as an escape route to flee from hunters.

"I waded out into the water and got the deer," Sauls recalled. "Although the deer was mortally wounded, and the hunter had made a good shot, we never would have recovered this deer without the Lab.

"If you plan to hunt swamps and flood plains anywhere, and you want to recover more of your animals, having a quality trailing dog is critical to your success."

One of the most unusual characteristics about a good trailing dog that works wetlands to find wounded bucks is its uncanny ability to locate and remain on the trail of a wounded deer even though there is no blood trail or apparent sign that the buck has been hit. In swampy regions with high deer populations, a trailing dog may cross over several fresh tracks that intersect the trail of the wounded deer. However, these dogs never seem to get off the trail of the buck that has been hit.

I've also found that neither rain, wind or elapsed time seem to keep a dog from being able to trail a wounded buck. Simmons' dog Sunny has recovered bucks even after the trail is more than eight-hours old and has gone through wet terrain. The trailing dogs I've seen in action appear to have a certain pride of workmanship about the way they do their tasks and are eager to find trails of wounded deer and relentless to stay on them to recover those animals.

What Factors Affect Wetland Hunting

However, not all wetlands or hunting situations are alike and not all of them require the services of a trailing dog. Hunting tactics vary along wetlands. But certain factors are consistent with taking quality bucks along flood plains.

* The biggest bucks in any swampy area often will be in the thickest cover, especially if the hunting pressure is intense in that region.

* You may have to take a shot at 30 yards or less in these thick-cover areas.

* The key to recovering a deer in wetlands may include employing the services of a trailing dog.

The fears of getting wet, becoming lost, encountering mosquitoes, redbugs, ticks, snakes and possibly alligators are what keep many deer hunters out of wetland regions. But overcome these fears, and try some of these strategies for wet-ground deer hunting. Then your chances of seeing more bucks and taking bigger bucks will be greatly increased this season.

CHAPTER 13

FIND MONSTER BUCKS IN CROPLANDS

As the buck ate moss off the side of a tree 150 yards away, all I could see was his head and his neck. A fallen tree shielded the rest of his body.

"Do you see him?" my guide, Norman LeBrun of Anticosti Island in Quebec, Canada, asked.

"I can see a part of him," I told LeBrun as I readied for the shot by bracing my Browning .243 on the side of a small spruce while I knelt in the snow.

"I don't think you can bag him from here, and we can't get any closer," LeBrun said.

A cleared field of snow was between the deer and us.

"I think I can take him," I whispered as I let out half of the deep breath I just had taken.

Although I knelt in the snow in Canada, the shot I had was the same one I had seen many times before in the soybean fields of south Alabama. The flat-shooting .243 with 100-grain Winchester bullets had dropped deer at 200 yards with only the deer's neck as a target before. I had every reason to believe the little gun would do the job it was designed to do -- shoot flat and accurately.

As the crosshairs in my Nikon 3-9X scope settled on the middle of the deer's out-stretched neck, I squeezed the trigger. At the report of the rifle, the 8-point buck went down.

"I don't believe you hit that deer," LeBrun observed as the report of my rifle faded in the distance. "I think he dropped and then ran off."

But when we arrived at the tree where the deer had been feeding, the buck was dead. The bullet had hit his spinal column and broken the animal's neck.

When you're hunting over crops and fields, whether the snow fields in Canada or soybean fields in Alabama, the same equipment for accurate shooting is required. Only the temperature varies. With a flat-shooting rifle, a quality scope and a cartridge that consistently shoots 1- to 2-inch groups, you can shoot with confidence at ranges of more than 100 yards in pastures and croplands.

Why Hunt Field and Pasture Bucks

Tad Brown of Warsaw, Missouri, has hunted pastures and croplands around his home for more than 20 years. He has developed strategies that regularly produce bucks at distances of 100 yards plus.

"I like to hunt green pastures," Brown explained. "Once I slipped up to the edge of a pasture where I'd seen deer previously. Using my binoculars, I spotted a group of deer at the other end of the field from me -- about 180 to 200 yards away. Hunting with a .270 Remington Model 700BDL rifle, I could pick up a nice-sized buck in my riflescope. I let the crosshairs settle behind the deer's front shoulder and squeezed the trigger. The buck went down immediately when my 130-grain Sierra Boattail hollow point hit him.

"I've tested many different bullets to determine which one shoots best in my rifle. The hollow point gives me good expansion when it goes through the ribs and does the damage required to dump the buck."

Brown sights in his rifle dead-on at 200 yards.

"By taking a long shot like this, the buck never saw, heard or smelled me," Brown emphasized. "The further you are away from the deer, the more likely you will be to bag him if you can shoot accurately."

At 100 yards, Brown's rifle will hit 2-1/2 to 3 inches high. At 300 yards, the bullet will land 2 inches low. At 400 yards, the bullet drop will be 10 to 12 inches. From 100 to 300 yards, Brown can hold dead-on and down a buck. With a deer at 400 yards, Brown settles his crosshairs on the deer's back and makes a heart or a lung shot. Brown prefers European-style reticles in his scope, which are wide coming

This non-typical trophy buck was only 4 years old and was taken near a soybean farm.

from the side of the scope and narrow toward the center of the scope where they cross. This kind of reticles gives him a finer aiming point.

According to Brown, in his home state of Missouri, most hunters prefer a .30-30 or a .30-06 for deer hunting. The vast majority of the hunters hunt woodlots instead of fields, which means less hunting pressure exists around the edges of the fields than in the woodlots. Where you find less hunting pressure, you usually locate more and bigger bucks.

"When I hunted in timber, I would see numbers of deer, but I couldn't get a shot off," Brown mentioned. "I'd either spot a white tail, a flash of antlers or a buck standing on the opposite side of the brush pile or a large tree.

"However, because of intense hunting pressure, I saw more bucks in the field and had the opportunity for a better shot than I ever had in the woods."

Brown also has discovered another advantage to field hunting. When he sits in a tree stand 15 to 20 feet off the ground and uses his binoculars and riflescope, he can see where the deer falls or which way the deer runs when he is hit. Brown then finds the buck quickly and recovers the animal much more easily than when he hunts in the woods.

How to Get Cropland to Hunt

In my home state of Alabama, deer sometimes are shot and left laying in the field to rot because of crop-deprivation permits. But Alabama is not the only state that issues these permits. Many states allow landowners to kill deer and leave them laying in the fields when the animals are destroying crops. The cropland hunter can be used as a management tool to control deer herds on croplands and often is welcomed by the landowner. In most farming regions, the deer the landowner wants to see gone the most are the antlerless deer. These animals represent the reproductive segment in the herd and are the least attractive to the hunter. The bucks have value, are the most desirable for hunting and will bring the biggest price to the landowner in the form of leasing his land to hunt.

By understanding the economical value of the deer that destroy the crops, you often can find good cropland to hunt. Here's how:

1) Check with your county extension agent and county conservation officer to see if any crop-deprivation permits have been given in your county or in the counties you want to hunt. Once you know which croplands have deer problems, you may locate a deer honeyhole.

2) Contact the landowner. Offer to take off the surplus of antlerless deer he needs removed, if he will let you hunt for bucks. Since the bucks have value, the landowner may offer the legal limit of bucks in exchange for your harvesting the antlerless deer. Discuss the antlerless harvest with the landowner and the conservation officer in the area you hunt. Often you will be able to donate the meat of these nuisance animals to some charity.

3) Learn where, how and when to hunt the croplands by removing the deer that are destroying the crops. You also will find the bucks you want to hunt when the season arrives. By solving the farmer's nuisance deer problem, you often can locate a productive place to hunt, provide food for the needy and locate big bucks to hunt later.

No one likes to see deer wasted, but the farmer has to protect his crops. By your becoming the management tool the farmers use for deer control, you often can find and bag the buck of your dreams.

You'll find a nice buck like this one often in a hayfield.

How Wind and Sun Affect Your Cropland Hunting

Since you're so far away from the animal when you take long-distance shots over crops, often the only way a deer detects you is when your human odor rides the wind. You must have the wind in your favor to watch fields and pastures for deer.

"I generally have several stands set up around the agricultural fields and the pastures I hunt," Brown commented. "By having more than one stand, then if the wind's wrong at my favorite stand, I still have another stand from which I can hunt. When hunters spot deer coming into a field from one direction, often they make the mistake of setting up their stands to only shoot in the direction from which they think the deer probably will enter the field. However, with a wrong wind, this stand will be totally useless."

Brown also chooses specific stands for morning hunting. He explained, "If you're looking into the sun, oftentimes you won't be able to see deer slipping through the fence or around the edge of a field

129

because the sun's blinding you. You also can pick up glare in your riflescope by facing into the sun, which can keep you from shooting accurately."

If you're hunting over a large field, a pasture, a clearcut or a powerline right-of-way as Brown does when he's long-range shooting, a Nikon spotting scope drastically can increase your ability to see deer -- especially early in the morning and late in the afternoon in low-light conditions. A spotting scope makes woodlots and fields appear brighter. Also utilizing a spotting scope enables you to remain well away from the deer to keep from spooking them and to watch where the bucks most often enter and exit the field.

Where to Look for Cropland Bucks

When hunting in pastures, greenfields, hay fields, wheat fields or any other type of agricultural crops where the foliage is no higher than the buck's knees and he is completely exposed as he crosses a field, you must know where to look for the buck, what he's going to do and when to take the shot.

Brown explained that, "A buck usually will cross a field at the most narrow point. When he makes the decision to go across the field, generally he'll move quickly. However, the deer gives you two opportunities to shoot.

"If you can spot the buck when he's walking just inside the timber at the edge of the field, often he'll stop, wait for a few minutes and survey the field before he crosses that open expanse. This time is the best to take your shot. Also field bucks may give you another chance to shoot. Just before entering the timber on the other side of the field, the bucks may stop and look into the woods before they move into the timber.

"If you take a shot at a buck and miss him when he's crossing a field, unless the bullet itself startles the deer, you're generally so far away from the animal, you may get a second shot. Or, if you shoot before the buck crosses the field and miss him, even if he sprints across the field, he'll often off you a second shot before he enters the timber on the other side."

Brown offers another tactic for stopping bucks crossing a field, even if they move quickly across the field. "I use my M.A.D. Quick Grunt, because it allows me to keep my hands on my gun and look through my scope at the same time. A buck only may pause for an instant on a field. As soon as you grunt and the deer stops, put your crosshairs behind the animal's shoulders and take the shot.

"I've tried to use conventional grunt tubes. But after I blow them to stop the deer, I have to put the grunt tube down, bring the rifle to my shoulder, find the deer in my scope, put the crosshairs in the kill zone and then take the shot. With the Quick Grunt, I can follow the deer in my scope, blow the grunt and as soon as the deer stops, I'm ready to shoot. I believe the hands-free type of grunt calls are a definite advantage when hunting bucks in pastures and fields."

What Other Crops and Food Deer Prefer

When using the word croplands, most hunters see visions of corn fields, winter wheat, oats, soybeans, peas, sweet potatoes and beets. In my home state of Alabama, croplands also means watermelon patches. Rarely do we think of orchards and pastures as croplands. However, apples, plums and pears also are on the deer's preferred food list.

Orchards offer easy deer-patterning opportunities. The first tree to drop fruit will be the tree the deer concentrate around first. But as the fruit begins to fall, if one tree produces better or sweeter fruit than the other trees do, the deer will feed under this tree more frequently.

Most hunters know if you pinpoint abandoned orchards you can find productive deer hunting, especially during the early deer season. To insure the most deer under the tree you want to hunt during the early season, fertilize one or two trees when hunting abandoned orchards before the tree's leaves form -- usually at the end of hunting season. Fertilize that same tree or trees during the early spring just as the leaves begin to show.

The fertilizer will cause these trees to bear more and sweeter-tasting fruit that the other trees in the old orchard. These special trees then will attract more deer than the other trees do and provide dependable stand sites for the bowhunter or early-season gun hunter.

Pastures that are fertilized also have an attracting power for deer. If you hunt where farmers raise livestock, the pastures frequently fertilized will produce more and sweeter grass than the pastures not fertilized. These fertilized pastures draw more deer than unfertilized pastures will.

Cornfields can produce nice-sized bucks like this one bagged by the author.

Greenfields that are planted for deer and other wildlife demonstrate this same attracting quality. The greenfields that are properly fertilized will draw more deer than the fields not fertilized.

How to Hunt Cropland Bucks

Bucks usually will move into croplands to feed late in the evening and go out of the crops early in the morning. However, after the crops have been harvested or if you hunt over pastures and greenfields, deer may cross these fields at any time of the day. Often the middle of the day is the best time to catch deer crossing agricultural fields, since that's when hunting pressure tends to be the lightest. The deer won't be as reluctant to move at that time.

To hunt an agricultural field early in the morning, plan to arrive at the field an hour before daylight. Climb into your tree stand as quietly as possible. Many hunters spook the deer they may have the chance to take because of making far too much noise going to their stands and climbing into their stands. Remember that sound carries a great distance in open country. Put your tree stand up the day before you plan to hunt. By allowing yourself more time than you think you need and getting into your stand before daylight, you'll climb much more quietly and take more time getting set up properly in the stand.

If you hunt in the afternoon, go to your stand two or three hours before dusk. Often hunters arrive at their stands too late, especially in the afternoons during the rut. Because big bucks chase does and move all day long during the rut, the likelihood of your seeing a trophy deer coming across a field and croplands can occur at any time.

Some years ago, I decided to hunt on the edge of a cornfield where the corn had been harvested early in the summer for roasting ears. The stalks had been cut down and left to rot in the field. Although the cornfield appeared to have nothing that would draw deer to it, some fresh young shoots of grass and weeds grew up between the rows. I discovered does feeding there.

By scouting the fields, I also pinpointed some well-defined trails and scrapes along the edges of the field. Knowing that bucks would appear at the scrape at almost any time during the rut and realizing the does already were feeding on the winter grass in the greenfield, I went to my stand at 1:00 p.m. As I slowly climbed the tree to reach my stand, I spotted movement about 75 yards away with my Nikon Mountaineer binoculars. A buck stood about 20 yards from his scrape eying a doe already out in the field.

As I tried to calm myself down, I noticed the buck looking in my direction. However, because the wind was in my favor and I remained motionless in my Trebark Universal camouflage, the deer never spotted me. I took my time and mounted my rifle. My rifle reported just as the buck took his first step out into the field. The buck fell.

Although dusk and dawn are the most productive times to take a white-tailed deer along agricultural fields during the rut, even when the crop has been harvested, you often can find bucks moving on the edges of abandoned fields where they leave scrapes and feed on grasses growing up after the crops have been harvested.

What Guns Are Best for Field Shooting

Although people often debate which calibers are best for long-distance shooting, Brown believes the .243, the 6mm, the .270 and the .225 are flat-shooting, low-recoil, easier-to-sight-in rifles than others on the market.

"Always consider the recoil of a rifle when choosing a gun with which to hunt over croplands," Brown emphasized. "If the gun kicks so much you anticipate the kick and flinch, you may pull your sights off the deer and miss. However, if you shoot a smaller caliber rifle and know where the bullet will hit at distances from 100 to 300 yards, you won't have to worry much about flinching."

My favorite guns for hunting deer over croplands at long ranges are the Browning .243 and the Remington 6mm. To see and bag more bucks this season, don't fight the crowds in the woods. Move to the fields or pastures. Use these strategies. You can bet on cropland bucks.

CHAPTER 14

HUNT LATE-SEASON PRESSURED BIG BUCKS

"Do you mount deer heads, fellow?" the overall-clad, snuff-dipping, older gentleman asked as he stood at the door of my taxidermy shop.

"Yes, sir, I do," I answered.

The man spit into the cup he had brought with him, looked up, smiled and said, "I got a couple I want to get mounted."

Excited to have business toward the end of deer season, I asked the man to bring the heads into my office. Because I assumed the deer either had been in the freezer or a cooler since the first of hunting season, I was quite surprised when the hunter came in with two, large, 8-point bucks that apparently were freshly killed.

"You must have a good hunting lease to take two fine bucks like these at the end of the season," I said with some surprise.

"Nope, I got them both on state wildlife management areas," the older hunter answered. "I usually take one to three bucks during the last two weeks of the season on state lands. Usually these bucks will have 6- to 8-points each, but one year I did get a 10-point buck."

I knew now this man was either one of the best late- season, public-land hunters I ever had met or a very convincing liar. I always had believed the best and biggest bucks on public lands were bagged at the

The place no one in his right mind will hunt is where you'll find a buck like this late in the season.

first of the season, certainly not at the very end of the season. At first the man was very secretive about his tactics. However, to stop me from asking so many questions, he finally agreed to tell me his public-land strategy.

Secrets to Late-Season Public-Land Bucks

"To take a nice buck at the end of the season on public lands, get into your tree stand before daylight," the old man explained with a smile. "Then remain in it until you take a buck or dark arrives. Carry your lunch and some plastic bags to use as portable potties."

But this simple answer did not satisfy my thirst to learn more. As I pried the details for successful late-season hunting for a big buck from this veteran woodsman, he smiled each time he gave up a secret.

"Generally, only three types of hunters hunt the late season -- the sportsman who has not bagged a buck, the outdoorsman who has one more deer tag to fill and the trophy hunter who has just about run out of time to take a monster-sized buck," the experienced hunter said. "All three groups of hunters have tremendous pressure exerted on them to find and take bucks. They feel they constantly must move to have success before the season ends, however, they generally will spook more deer than they ever see. "When everyone else in the woods moves, climb into your tree stand, and sit there all day long. Then you will be the only person not moving in the woods."

This hunter was convinced that his remaining on his stand while all the other hunters walked around or went up and down trees changing stand sites drove deer to him.

"Get as far away as you can from the road," he insisted. "Locate the best thick cover 1/2 to 1-1/2 miles away from where other hunters will enter the woods. When you find a spot for your tree stand, realize you only must be able to see 20 to 50 yards to take a buck. Learn to use your compass to get back to your car and return to that tree stand before daylight. Then the next morning before first light, be in that stand waiting on your buck."

As I listened carefully, the old hunter told me to expect to see bucks in the thickets just at first light when most of the other hunters were coming into the woods.

"The bucks will move into the thickets then to escape hunting pressure. They know when they hear car doors slam and hunters walking that to survive they must go into that thick cover.

"In the middle of the day, when the hunters leave the woods to eat lunch, the bucks often will move out of the thick cover to feed and breed and then return to the thick cover when the hunters reenter the woods. Just at dark when hunters begin to leave the woods, again the bucks will come from the heavy cover into more open areas.

"Also remember, deer are browsers and like to walk around much of the time. Even though they may be in thick cover during most of the daylight hours, at the end of the season they will not be lying down sleeping all day long. The bucks will stand up, walk around, feed and even breed their does in these remote areas. The more time you spend in a tree stand in thick cover on public lands, the better your chances will be for bagging a buck in the late season."

Private-Land Strategies for Late-Season Bucks

Hunting over greenfields is a very successful method for bagging bucks in the South and is where most of the deer hunting done in January is available. However, after the first three weeks of deer season, many of the bucks, especially the older-age-class bucks, have discovered that the most hunting pressure is exerted on these fields from before daylight until 10:00 a.m. and from 2:00 p.m. until dark. In response to this hunting pressure, the bucks often feed on greenfields and meet does in these regions in the middle of the day and after dark, which are the safest times for them to frequent these fields.

I surveyed five hunting clubs in my section of the South. Each club reported they took some of the biggest bucks of the year on their club's greenfields late in the season.

But many hunters are not willing to give up their lunches and their midday naps to sit over greenfields in the middle of the afternoon. However, late in the season, hunting these greenfields at these times of day often will be where you will find the largest bucks.

I tested this theory of hunting late-season bucks on private lands at midday a few years ago. The sun was warm. I could feel my eyelids pulling down like window shades. I had eaten one too many sandwiches for lunch and was comfortable in my Warren and Sweat tree stand. The usual fear of falling out of the tree was now gone as I was held securely to the trunk by my Brell-Mar harness. I had been in the tree since first light. I had looked at every tree, each stick and every blade of grass at least a thousand times. I was bored. But I had made the decision to remain in the tree until I bagged my buck or darkness enveloped me.

I employed a strategy I had developed years ago of half- sleeping -- a state of semi-consciousness where I opened one eye and peeped out every five minutes or so. Since I didn't fully commit both eyes to the task of looking for deer, I wouldn't totally wake up. Utilizing this tactic, I could halfway sleep and halfway hunt at the same time without making a total commitment to either.

When the sun was at its zenith, my reverie was broken by the raspy barking of a fox squirrel on the edge of the greenfield. I sat up straight. In the brush, I spotted a parallel line about 3 feet off the ground where I had seen no limb or bush before. I closed my eyes again as I considered what I had seen. Was that line the back of a deer or just a hallucination from the depths of my half-sleep? Not wanting to wake up but realizing I was supposed to be hunting, I committed both eyes to looking where I had seen the line.

The object moved. A deer stood not 40 yards away from me on the edge of the cover. I straightened my back and picked up my Nikon

You won't catch monster bucks like this one strolling in the open during hunting season -- (Drawing by Jim Tostrud).

Mountaineer binoculars to get a better look at the animal. As I watched through my binoculars, I saw a patch of brown and then a white tail swish. The buck in front of me was looking toward the greenfield.

A surge of adrenaline chased all thought of sleep into a speedy retreat as I mounted my Winchester 7mm Mag and readied for the shot. I found a small clearing in the brush the buck should pass through before he entered the greenfield. That clearing was where I planned to take the shot.

The buck had 4 points on one side of his rack and an undetermined number on the other. Finally the buck stepped into my shooting lane. Quickly my crosshairs found a spot just behind the buck's shoulder where I wanted the bullet to land. Slowly and steadily I squeezed the trigger until I heard the explosion. I listened to the buck fall and thrash in the brush. I waited 30 minutes and then left my tree stand and found my 7-point buck.

Bucks in Weird Places

A small island sat in the middle of an oxbow lake just off the Tombigbee River in west-central Alabama and was part of a hunting club I had belonged to for years. For hunters to reach the island, we had to walk 3/4-mile, carrying boats and canoes through the woods, and then paddle across the lake. Hunting the island was a two-day ordeal.

Usually on the first day we carried the boats through the woods, tied them up on the edge of the bank and then returned to camp. The second day we climbed out of our beds two hours before daylight, walked through the woods to the boats, paddled across the lake quietly and put out standers on one end of the island and drivers on the other part of the island. Just at first light, the drivers slowly and softly would start walking down the island toward the standers.

Because the hunt on the island was such a major undertaking, we never hunted on the island until the end of the season. But we often harvested one to four bucks on that one-day-a-year hunt.

Big bucks frequent sanctuaries like islands and other out-of-the-way places where no one hunts during the late season. One of the best ways to find older-age-class bucks a the end of the season is by using either an aerial photo or a topographical map of the property you plan to hunt. Study the property carefully. Begin to look for places that haven't been hunted all season long.

In the South, one of the best regions to find late-season bucks is cotton fields. Because these fields appear to offer little cover, no one thinks of looking for deer there during daylight hours. But these fields provide ideal hideouts for deer. If you fly over these fields in airplanes, you'll often see big bucks holding in the cotton fields.

Another late-season hotspot for deer is small drainage ditches in agricultural fields. Although the fields may be barren of crops, the ditches may have brush on the edges. By laying in the ditch, a buck can see for 100 to 200 yards in all directions.

You may locate bucks late in the season along woods roads leading to the hunting camp -- perhaps within 150 yards of the camp. Most hunters never hunt from the edge of the road that leads to the camp because they think cars going up and down the road spook any deer holding there.

However, at the end of last season, a friend and I discovered a tremendous racked buck not 20 yards from a major interstate. Ten-year-old planted pines lined the edge of the interstate. We walked along the edge of the planted pine and found scrapes and rubs. The pines stopped at a creek, which meandered through a hardwood bottom. Once we pinpointed the deer's scrape line, we saw where he was bedded in the pines immediately beside the interstate, moving along the creek bottom and feeding in the acorn flat next to the creek.

Bucks become accustomed to highway traffic and soon learn vehicles pose no threat to their survival. When searching for a late-season trophy buck, scout areas close to where cars and trucks move through the woods or along the edge of woodlots but where no hunters hunt.

Most sportsmen never consider finding a trophy buck right behind a camphouse or farmhouse. But remember, older-age-class bucks learn to move away from hunting pressure into areas where they feel little or no pressure.

One of the biggest bucks ever brought into my taxidermy shop was taken in a region like this. The man who bagged the buck told me, ''Our club has a dog pen 50 yards behind our clubhouse where we keep the bird dogs and beagles we hunt with after deer season. Behind the dog pen is a briar thicket.

"One morning I got up before daylight. While I was sipping my coffee in the upstairs bedroom, I thought I saw an antler move in that briar thicket. Since I'd only had one swallow of my coffee, I thought I was probably dreaming. I decided to take my shotgun and walk behind the dog pen.

"The wind blew in my face and the dogs barked when I started into the briars. When I'd only gone about 10 yards, the biggest buck I'd ever seen stood up and looked at me. As he turned to run, I mounted my 3-inch Magnum. The slug found the target behind his shoulder. The deer made three jumps and dropped on the other side of the briars. Most of the other men in the camp, who were still having breakfast when they heard the shotgun report, came running out of the house to see what had happened. No one could believe I'd shot that big buck by the dog pen.

"But as we discussed why the deer was there, we all agreed that that spot was the only place on the property we hadn't hunted and wouldn't hunt because we believed the barking dogs kept any deer away. Apparently this buck had learned from several seasons of dodging hunting pressure that the briar patch behind the dog pen was a safe haven, because we never had seen this buck on the property before.

"When we aged the buck, we discovered he was 6 years old. He must have been hiding in the briar patch behind that dog pen for many years."

I met a mystery buck a few years ago at Bent Creek Lodge near Jachin, Alabama. Although the buck sometimes appeared on the edge of a creek beside the road leading in to the lodge, no one seemed to be able to pattern the buck. He would show up at daylight and then vanish without leaving a trace. One day I went down to the bridge, which was less than 200 yards from the camphouse, and crossed the small stream where we usually saw the buck. Along the edge of the bank I found a well-worn deer trail. That evening, I had to leave to go home. However, I told a friend of mine about the buck. Before daylight the next morning, he sat on his tree stand near the trail with his bow.

He told me later, "John, I couldn't believe it. The buck came under the bridge just like you said he would. He walked in the creek up beside my stand. I took the shot at less than 15 yards. The deer was a nice 8 point. I'm convinced he stayed in that creek to leave no sign going to wherever he found his does and/or food."

142

Often if you have a steady wind blowing to hide the sound of your movements, you can go into thick-cover bedding areas and bag a trophy buck.

Love on the Move

If you hunt in a state where the rut occurs during the late season, then scrape hunting will be deadly effective. However, understanding when to hunt what scrapes is the key to finding late-season bucks. Some bucks works their open scrapes like those along the edges of logging roads or fields only after dark and come looking for love in their thick-cover scrapes during daylight hours.

But when I asked Dr. Larry Marchinton, professor of wildlife science at the University of Georgia, where he would hunt during the late season, he explained, "I believe the best place to hunt at any time of the year is a funnel area - - a region especially productive for bucks during the rut. A funnel is where two different types of terrain come close together with either a woodlot or some type of thick cover between them.

"For instance, if a creek bend and a field corner close to each other with a narrow strip of woods between these two points and a large block of hardwoods on either end, this site is a funnel area. During the late season, if you can find scrapes on both ends of the funnel, you have a good chance of seeing a buck walking through the funnel going from one

143

scrape to the other scrape. In funnel areas during the late season, I generally see more deer than at any other spot I hunt.''

Yet another strategy for taking late-season bucks looking for love is to know when to hunt a scrape.

According to Donald Spence, a very successful veteran deer hunter with both primitive and conventional weapons, ''Most hunters spook the bucks they're trying to take when they hunt scrapes because they go to the scrapes just at daylight. Bucks most likely will come to their scrapes just at first light. You must be on your stand watching the scrape before the sun comes up to bag these bucks.

''Remember to look behind your stand frequently. Many times a buck will come near a scrape and then circle downwind to try to pick up the smell of a doe that is close to the scrape. When you watch a scrape, look not only for the buck to come down the trail leading to the scrape but also expect to see the buck downwind of the scrape.''

Most of the biggest bucks taken at the end of the season are by sportsmen who've learned how and where to hunt late-season bucks. These bucks are the smartest whitetails because they have dodged hunters all season long. To take these older-age-class bucks, break with the traditional hunting tactics, and search for these trophies in overlooked places.

CHAPTER 15

BEWARE OF HUMAN ODOR WHEN HUNTING BIG BUCKS

The whitetail deer's number one defense system is its sense of smell. If a whitetail buck smells you, he'll usually leave the area before you can see him. The most critical key to successful deer hunting is to rid your hunt site of human odor. The more human odor you can eliminate from the area you hunt, the greater your odds will be for taking a buck.

Although many manufacturers promise products that completely dispose of human odor, the only person who effectively has been able to totally eliminate human odor is the undertaker. The only surefire way to eliminate human odor from your hunt site is to always hunt into the wind. The body constantly produces odor. As pores breathe, they give off odor. The more heat generated by the body, the more odor the body emits. Even though we can't stop our bodies from producing odor, we can reduce the amount of odor our bodies give off.

The First Line of Defense

Odor occurs on the skin when amino acids come to the top layer of skin. This odor has a residual effect much like suntan lotion does when it is applied to the body. Even after the lotion appears to have dried, a film of the lotion lies on the upper surface of the skin. Body odor too lies on the skin after seeping out through the pores.

To begin to eliminate human odor, the hunter must bathe before he hunts. Because soap manufacturers realize human odor is on the skin's

By using an odor neutralizer like Scent Blaster by Buckstop, the author bagged this deer, even though the buck came in from downwind.

surface, they add some type of perfume to their soaps. Then the soap not only cleans the odor and the sweat residue off the skin but also leaves a distinctive smell on the skin.

However, a perfumed smell can spook deer as effectively as human odor when hunting. The thinking hunter will use some of the new body soaps formulated by the scent industry which clean the skin, do not have a perfumed smell and leave a residue of odor-neutralizing chemicals on the surface of the skin.

Products like Berkley's Sportsman's Soap and Scent Shield's Body Soap help neutralize or encapsulate odor as it rises to the upper layer of the skin by leaving a film on the skin. However, this layer of odor-neutralizing or encapsulating product can be saturated or washed away with perspiration. If you only use a body soap, you have a limited amount of odor protection. Utilizing a second layer of defense to increase the length of time you neutralize or encapsulate body odor is very important to success afield.

146

A trophy buck like this one uses his nose more than his eyes or ears to avoid the hunter.

The Second Line of Defense

When the first layer of defense on the skin is broken down or saturated, the second line of defense is the sportsman's clothes. Many products on the market today like Tink's No Stink from Wellington Outdoors not only clean your clothes and wash the odor out of them without leaving a perfumed smell in the clothes but also add an odor-neutralizing agent to your clothing. When your first layer of defense against odor breaks down, you have a second layer of defense in the odor neutralizers in your clothes that acts as a barrier against human odor. You've doubled your protection and increased your odds for a buck's not smelling you.

The Third Line of Defense

The third layer of defense is a hotspot spray -- a spray-on with increased chemical intensity that neutralizes odor. Spray this product on the outside of your clothing in the areas where the most human odor is produced like your hat, armpits, crotch, behind your knees and on your feet. This additional chemical protection offers a third and stronger barrier through which odor must pass to escape into the air.

You can know the wind's direction by using a string and a compass. When you're hunting trophy bucks, don't go into your hunt site if you know the wind is blowing from the wrong direction.

The Fourth Line Defense

Some excellent research has been performed on how to best neutralize breath odor. If we eliminate body odor without ridding ourselves of breath odor, we've only solved half our problem. Although plenty of mouthwashes and breath sprays are on the market today, just like the soap, the odor neutralizing chemicals found in these products also tend to add a perfume-type smell to make the breath smell sweet. A sweet smell will spook as many deer as bad breath will. Although hunters realize what they eat is what they smell like, carefully avoiding strong smelling foods for the duration of deer season often is impossible -- especially when you live in a state like my home state of Alabama which has a 3 1/2-month-long deer season.

When a buck smells human odor, he'll generally leave an area.

Two companies have developed products to try and neutralize or camouflage breath odor. Wellington Outdoors produces Tink's Breath Camo, a liquid the hunter gargles to neutralize breath odor and reduce the likelihood of the deer picking up this odor. Golden Eagle Archery makes a chewing gum to neutralize breath odor that has a vanilla-flavored smell that is touted to help attract deer.

The Fifth Line of Defense

Behind the knees and the soles of the feet are two areas of the body which produce a large amount of body odor. Even with four layers of defense, these two regions can generate so much perspiration that your chemical defense system can be broken down and defeated. However, if you wear hip waders, you can encapsulate these body parts in a rubber coating that prevents human odor from escaping. Because trappers have realized this fact for many years, most trappers usually wear hip waders when running a trap line.

Another advantage of wearing hip waders -- or even chest-high waders -- is you can walk through water without getting wet. Your feet and your legs will stay cooler, you won't leave any odor in the water, and you'll reduce the amount of sound you make as you travel through the woods, if you move slowly enough. The more often you can use water as a vehicle to move through woods, the less likely you are to leave any scent in the woods, and the greater your odds are for bagging a buck.

The Effects of the Wind

Although odor eliminators or neutralizers can reduce the likelihood of deer downwind of you smelling you, your odor is less likely to be detected by a deer when you hunt from a tree stand in the morning. On a still day with little or no wind, human odor moves upward with the thermals (wind currents) that come from the ground and rise to the sky.

A downward thermal, which is a downward movement of air currents, usually occurs when you hunt in the afternoons. Deer will be less likely to smell you if you hunt from a ground blind in the afternoons.

Scientists do not know exactly how much human odor deer can smell. For instance, can a deer smell one part in 100, or can he smell one part in one million? Once we know the amount of human odor a deer can smell, then the scent and lure industry will be able to produce better products to more effectively reduce human odor and help hunters spook fewer deer.

Index

A

aerial photo   29, 99
amino acids   145
Anticosti Island   78, 107, 125

B

Benoit, Larry   80
Bent Creek Lodge   108, 142
Boone & Crockett   48
Bostick Plantation   117
Brown, Carl   41
Brown, Tad   126

C

Cackle   39
Carlson, Noble   86
Carlton, Wayne   39
Causey, Dr. Keith   43
computer   106

D

Demarais, Steve   24
dominant buck   44

E

estrus   15
European-style reticles   126

F

funnel   102, 143

G

grunt tube   39, 74, 131

H

Haydel, Rod   69

J

Jacobson, Harry   25

K

Keck, Rob   41
Koerth, Ben   22
Kroll, James   22

L

LeBrun, Norman   77, 108, 125
limb breaking   72

M

man-drive   113
Marchinton, Dr. Larry   143
McMillan, Ed   89
mineral blocks   97
Morse Code   41

N

Nelson, Dr. Jim 47
nocturnal 14, 23
Norton, Larry 108

O

odor eliminators or
      neutralizers 150

P

Pitman, Bo 29, 100

R

radio telemetry 20, 25
radio-collared 24
rattling antlers 72
Rongstad, Orrin J. 19
Russell, Delana 48

S

Sauls, Perry 122
scent trail 92
Sheppard, Dr. Robert 105
Simmons, Hayward 119
Spence, Donald 59, 144
Spence, Jody 61
subordinate buck 44

T

thermals 150
topo map 99
topographical maps 30

U

U. S. Geological Survey 101
Using a Drag 110

W

Warner, Steve 69
Webb, Braz 116

Y

Yeoman, Chris 39, 47

Z

Zaiglin, Bob 22

BASS SERIES LIBRARY
by Larry Larsen

(BSL1) FOLLOW THE FORAGE - BASS/PREY RELATIONSHIP - Learn how to determine dominant forage in a body of water and catch more bass!

(BSL2) VOL. 2 BETTER BASS ANGLING TECHNIQUES - Learn why one lure or bait is more successful than others and how to use each lure under varying conditions.

(BSL3) BASS PRO STRATEGIES - Professional fishermen know how changes in pH, water level, temperature and color affect bass fishing, and they know how to adapt to weather and topographical variations. Learn from their experience.

(BSL4) BASS LURES - TRICKS & TECHNIQUES - When bass become accustomed to the same artificials and presentations seen over and over again, they become harder to catch. You will learn how to modify your lures and rigs and how to develop new presentation and retrieve methods to spark the interest of largemouth!

(BSL5) SHALLOW WATER BASS - Bass spend 90% of their time in waters less than 15 feet deep. Learn productive new tactics that you can apply in marshes, estuaries, reservoirs, lakes, creeks and small ponds, and you'll triple your results!

HAVE THEM ALL!
"Larry, I'm ordering one book to give a friend for his birthday and your two new ones. I have all the BASS SERIES LIBRARY except one, otherwise I would have ordered an autographed set. I have followed your writings for years and consider them the best of the best!"
J. Vinson, Cataula, GA

(BSL6) BASS FISHING FACTS - Learn why and how bass behave during pre- and post-spawn, how they utilize their senses when active and how they respond to their environment, and you'll increase your bass angling success!

(BSL7) TROPHY BASS - If you're more interested in wrestling with one or two monster largemouth than with a "panful" of yearlings, then learn what techniques and locations will improve your chances.

TWO TROPHIES!
"By using your techniques and reading your Bass Series Library of books, I was able to catch the two biggest bass I've ever caught!"
B. Conley, Cromwell, IN

(BSL8) ANGLER'S GUIDE TO BASS PATTERNS - Catch bass every time out by learning how to develop a productive pattern quickly and effectively. "Bass Patterns" is a reference source for all anglers, regardless of where they live or their skill level. Learn how to choose the right lure, presentation and habitat under various weather and environmental conditions!

(BSL9) BASS GUIDE TIPS - Learn secret techniques known only in a certain region or state that often work in waters all around the country. It's this new approach that usually results in excellent bass angling success. Learn how to apply what the country's top guides know!

Nine Great Volumes To Help You Catch More and Larger Bass!

(LB1) LARRY LARSEN ON BASS TACTICS

is the ultimate "how-to" book that focuses on proven productive methods. **Hundreds of highlighted tips and drawings in our LARSEN ON BASS SERIES explain how you**

can catch more and larger bass in waters all around the country. This reference source by America's best known bass fishing writer will be invaluable to both the avid novice and expert angler!

(PF1) PEACOCK BASS EXPLOSIONS! by Larry Larsen

A must read for those anglers who are interested in catching the world's most exciting fresh water fish! Detailed tips, trip planning and tactics for peacocks in South Florida, Venezuela, Brazil, Puerto Rico, Hawaii and other destinations. This book explores the most effective tactics to take the aggressive peacock bass. You'll learn how to catch

more and larger fish using the valuable information from the author and expert angler, a four-time peacock bass world-record holder. It's the first comprehensive discussion on this wild and colorful fish.

BASS WATERS GUIDE SERIES by Larry Larsen

The most productive bass waters are described in this multi-volume series, including boat ramps, seasonal tactics, water characteristics and more. Numerous maps and photos detail specific locations.

(BW1) GUIDE TO NORTH FLORIDA BASS WATERS - Covers from Orange Lake north and west. Includes Lakes Lochloosa, Talquin and Seminole, the St. Johns, Nassau, Suwannee and Apalachicola Rivers; Newnans Lake, St. Mary's River, Juniper Lake, Ortega River, Lake Jackson, Deer Point Lake, Panhandle Mill Ponds and many more!

(BW2) GUIDE TO CENTRAL FLORIDA BASS WATERS - Covers from Tampa/Orlando to Palatka. Includes Lakes George, Rodman, Monroe, Tarpon and the Harris Chain, the St. Johns, Oklawaha and Withlacoochee Rivers, the Ocala Forest, Crystal River, Hillsborough River, Conway Chain, Homosassa River,

Lake Minneola, Lake Weir, Lake Hart, Spring Runs and many more!

(BW3) GUIDE TO SOUTH FLORIDA BASS WATERS - Covers from I-4 to the Everglades. Includes Lakes Tohopekaliga, Kissimmee, Okeechobee, Poinsett, Tenoroc and Blue Cypress, the Winter Haven Chain, Fellsmere Farm 13. Caloosahatchee River, Lake June-in-Winter, the Everglades, Lake Istokpoga, Peace River, Crooked Lake, Lake Osborne, St. Lucie Canal, Shell Creek, Lake Marian, Lake Pierce, Webb Lake and many more!

OUTDOOR TRAVEL SERIES
by Larry Larsen and M. Timothy O'Keefe

Candid guides on the best charters, time of the year, and other recommendations that can make your next fishing and/or diving trip much more enjoyable.

(OT1) FISH & DIVE THE CARIBBEAN - Vol. 1 Northern Caribbean, including Cozumel, Cayman Islands, Bahamas, Jamaica, Virgin Islands. Required reading for fishing and diving enthusiasts who want to know the most cost-effective means to enjoy these and other Caribbean islands.

(OT3) FISH & DIVE FLORIDA & The Keys - Where and how to plan a vacation to America's most popular fishing and diving destination. Features include artificial reef loran numbers; freshwater springs/caves; coral reefs/barrier islands; gulf stream/passes; inshore flats/channels; and back country estuaries.

> **BEST BOOK CONTENT!**
> *"Fish & Dive the Caribbean" was a finalist in the Best Book Content Category of the National Association of Independent Publishers (NAIP). Over 500 books were submitted by publishers including Simon & Schuster and Turner Publishing. Said the judges "An excellent source book with invaluable instructions. Written by two nationally-known experts who, indeed, know what vacationing can be!"*

DIVING SERIES by M. Timothy O'Keefe

(DL1) DIVING TO ADVENTURE shows how to get started in underwater photography, how to use current to your advantage, how to avoid seasickness, how to dive safely after dark, and how to plan a dive vacation, including live-aboard diving.

(DL2) MANATEES - OUR VANISHING MERMAIDS is an in-depth overview of nature's strangest-looking, gentlest animals. They're among America's most endangered mammals. The book covers where to see manatees while diving, why they may be living fossils, their unique life cycle, and much more.

UNCLE HOMER'S OUTDOOR CHUCKLE BOOK
by Homer Circle, Fishing Editor, Sports Afield

(OC1) In his inimitable humorous style, "Uncle Homer" relates jokes, tales, personal anecdotes and experiences covering several decades in the outdoors. These stories, memories and moments will bring grins, chuckles and deep down belly laughs as you wend your way through the folksy copy and cartoons. If you appreciate the lighter side of life, this book is a must!

OUTDOOR ADVENTURE LIBRARY
by Vin T. Sparano, Editor-in-Chief, Outdoor Life

(OA1) HUNTING DANGEROUS GAME - Live the adventure of hunting those dangerous animals that hunt back! Track a rogue elephant, survive a grizzly attack, and face a charging Cape buffalo. These classic tales will make you very nervous next time you're in the woods!

> **KEEP ME UPDATED!**
> *"I would like to get on your mailing list. I really enjoy your books!"*
> G. Granger, Cypress, CA

(OA2) GAME BIRDS & GUN DOGS - A unique collection of tales about hunters, their dogs and the upland game and waterfowl they hunt. You will read about good gun dogs and heart-breaking dogs, but never about bad dogs, because there's no such animal.

COASTAL FISHING GUIDES
by Frank Sargeant

A unique "where-to" series of detailed secret spots for Florida's finest saltwater fishing. These guide books describe hundreds of little-known honeyholes and exactly how to fish them. Prime seasons, baits and lures, marinas and dozens of detailed maps of the prime spots are included. The comprehensive index helps the reader to further pinpoint productive areas and tactics. Over $160 worth of personally-marked NOAA charts in the two books.

(FG1) FRANK SARGEANT'S SECRET SPOTS Tampa Bay to Cedar Key Covers Hillsborough River and Davis Island through the Manatee River, Mullet Key and the Suwannee River.

(FG2) FRANK SARGEANT'S SECRET SPOTS Southwest Florida Covers from Sarasota Bay to Marco.

INSHORE SERIES
by Frank Sargeant

(IL1) THE SNOOK BOOK-"Must" reading for anyone who loves the pursuit of this unique sub-tropic species. Every aspect of how you can find and catch big snook is covered, in all seasons and all waters where snook are found.

(IL2) THE REDFISH BOOK-Packed with expertise from the nation's leading redfish anglers and guides, this book covers every aspect of finding and fooling giant reds. You'll learn secret techniques revealed for the first time. After reading this informative book, you'll catch more redfish on your next trip!

(IL3) THE TARPON BOOK-Find and catch the wily "silver king" along the Gulf Coast, north through the mid-Atlantic, and south along Central and South American coastlines. Numerous experts share their most productive techniques.

(IL4) THE TROUT BOOK-Jammed with tips from the nation's leading trout guides and light tackle anglers. For both the old salt and the rank amateur who pursue the spotted weakfish, or seatrout, throughout the coastal waters of the Gulf and Atlantic.

HUNTING LIBRARY
by John E. Phillips

(DH1) MASTERS' SECRETS OF DEER HUNTING - Increase your deer hunting success by learning from the masters of the sport. New information on tactics and strategies is included in this book, the most comprehensive of its kind.

(DH2) THE SCIENCE OF DEER HUNTING Covers why, where and when a deer moves and deer behavior. Find the answers to many of the toughest deer hunting problems a sportsman ever encounters!

(DH3) MASTERS' SECRETS OF BOW-HUNTING DEER - Learn the skills required to take more bucks with a bow, even during gun season. A must read for those who walk into the woods with a strong bow and a swift shaft.

(DH4) HOW TO TAKE MONSTER BUCKS - Specific techniques that will almost guarantee a trophy buck next season! Includes tactics by some of the nation's most accomplished trophy buck hunters.

> **RECOMMENDATION!**
> *"Masters' Secrets of Turkey Hunting is one of the best books around. If you're looking for a good turkey book, buy it!"*
> J. Spencer, Stuttgart Daily Leader, AR
>
> **NO BRAGGIN'!**
> *"From anyone else Masters' Secrets of Deer Hunting would be bragging and unbelievable. But not with John Phillips, he's paid his dues!"* F. Snare, Brookville Star, OH

(TH1) MASTERS' SECRETS OF TURKEY HUNTING - Masters of the sport have solved some of the most difficult problems you can encounter while hunting wily longbeards with bows, blackpowder guns and shotguns. Learn the 10 deadly sins of turkey hunting.

(BP1) BLACKPOWDER HUNTING SECRETS - Learn how to take more game during and after the season with black powder guns. If you've been hunting with black powder for years, this book will teach you better tactics to use throughout the year.

FISHING LIBRARY

(CF1) MASTERS' SECRETS OF CRAPPIE FISHING by John E. Phillips Learn how to make crappie start biting again once they have stopped, select the best jig color, find crappie in a cold front, through the ice, or in 100-degree heat. Unusual, productive crappie fishing techniques are included.

(CF2) CRAPPIE TACTICS by Larry Larsen - This book will improve your catch! The book includes some basics for fun fishing, advanced techniques for year 'round crappie and tournament preparation.

> **CRAPPIE COUP!**
> *"After reading your crappie book, I'm ready to overthrow the 'crappie king' at my lakeside housing development!"*
> R. Knorr, Haines City, FL

(CF3) MASTERS' SECRETS OF CATFISHING by John E. Phillips is your best guide to catching the best-tasting, elusive cats. Learn the best time of the year, the most productive places and which states to fish in your pursuit of Mr. Whiskers.

LARSEN'S OUTDOOR PUBLISHING
CONVENIENT ORDER FORM
ALL PRICES INCLUDE POSTAGE/HANDLING

FRESH WATER
___BSL1. Better Bass Angling Vol 1 ($11.95)
___BSL2. Better Bass Angling Vol 2 ($11.95)
___BSL3. Bass Pro Strategies ($11.95)
___BSL4. Bass Lures/Techniques ($11.95)
___BSL5. Shallow Water Bass ($11.95)
___BSL6. Bass Fishing Facts ($11.95)
___BSL7. Trophy Bass ($11.95)
___BSL8. Bass Patterns ($11.95)
___BSL9. Bass Guide Tips ($11.95)
___CF1. Mstrs' Scrts/Crappie Fshng ($11.95)
___CF2. Crappie Tactics ($11.95)
___CF3. Mstr's Secrets of Catfishing ($11.95)
___LB1. Larsen on Bass Tactics ($14.95)
___PF1. Peacock Bass Explosions! ($14.95)

SALT WATER
___IL1.   The Snook Book ($11.95)
___IL2.   The Redfish Book ($11.95)
___IL3.   The Tarpon Book ($11.95)
___IL4.   The Trout Book ($11.95)

OTHER OUTDOORS BOOKS
___DL1. Diving to Adventure ($11.95)
___DL2. Manatees/Vanishing ($10.95)
___OC1. Uncle Homer's Outdoor
            Chuckle Book ($9.95)

REGIONAL
___FG1.   Secret Spots-Tampa Bay/
            Cedar Key   ($14.95)
___FG2.   Secret Spots - SW Florida ($14.95)
___BW1. Guide/North Fl. Waters ($14.95)
___BW2. Guide/Cntral Fl.Waters ($14.95)
___BW3. Guide/South Fl.Waters ($14.95)
___OT1.   Fish/Dive - Caribbean   ($13.95)
___OT3.   Fish/Dive Florida/ Keys ($13.95)

HUNTING
___DH1. Mstrs' Secrets/ Deer Hunting ($11.95)
___DH2. Science of Deer Hunting ($11.95)
___DH3. Mstrs' Secrets/Bowhunting ($11.95)
___DH4. How to Take Monster Bucks ($13.95)
___TH1. Mstrs' Secrets/ Turkey Hunting ($11.95)
___OA1. Hunting Dangerous Game! ($11.95)
___OA2. Game Birds & Gun Dogs ($11.95)
___BP1. Blackpowder Hunting Secrets ($13.95)

VIDEO &
SPECIAL DISCOUNT PACKAGES
___ V1 - Video - Advanced Bass Tactics $24.95
___ BSL - Bass Series Library (9 vol. set) $79.95
___ IL - Inshore Library (4 vol. set) $35.95
___ BW - Guides to Bass Waters (3 vols.) $37.95
Volume sets are autographed by each author.

> **BIG SAVINGS!**
> **2-3 books, discount 10%**
> **4 or more books, discount 20%**

> **INTERNATIONAL ORDERS**
> **Send check in U.S. funds; add**
> **$2more per book for airmail rate**

ALL PRICES INCLUDE POSTAGE/HANDLING

No. of books _____ *x $*____ *ea = $*_____   *Special Package* _____ *@ $*_____
No. of books _____ *x $*____ *ea = $*_____   *Special Package* _____ *@ $*_____
No. of books _____ *x $*____ *ea = $*_____   *Video (50-min) $24.95 = $*_____
    SUBTOTAL   *$*_____   *SUBTOTAL*   *$*_____

*__Multi-book Discount__ (%) $*_____   *(N/A on discount packages or video)*

TOTAL ENCLOSED (check or money order)   *$*_____

*NAME*_____ *ADDRESS*_____

*CITY*_____*STATE*_____ *ZIP*_____

Send check or Money Order to: Larsen's Outdoor Publishing, Dept. RD95
2640 Elizabeth Place, Lakeland, FL 33813 (813)644-3381

ADDITIONAL BOOKS FROM OUR FRIENDS AT ...NIGHT HAWK PUBLICATIONS

Please send me the following books (prices include postage & handling)

_____ **DEER & FIXINGS COOKBOOK** by John & Denise Phillips. More than 50 years combined experience in preparing venison, a heart-smart meat with fewer calories and less fat and cholesterol but more protein than chicken, contains information on field and home care of venison as well as more than 100 proven venison recipes and more than 100 recipes for side dishes to accompany venison. **$15.50 each**

_____ **OUTDOOR LIFE'S COMPLETE TURKEY HUNTING** by John E. Phillips includes the newest tactics from more than 35 of the best turkey hunters across the nation for hunting gobblers as well as more than 180 drawings and photos. **$27.95 each.**

_____ **FISH & FIXINGS COOKBOOK** by John & Denise Phillips For all heart and health-conscious outdoorsmen, more than 125 delicious recipes for grilling, broiling, baking and frying saltwater and freshwater fish. More than 125 recipes for side dishes and numerous tips on handling fresh and frozen fish. **$15.50 each**

_____ **TURKEY TACTICS** by John E. Phillips Part of the North American Hunting Club's Library, this comprehensive book covers the biology and habits of the wild turkey and gives a vast array of strategies for bagging them. **$21.50 each**

_____ **DOUBLEDAY'S TURKEY HUNTER'S BIBLE** by John E. Phillips This widely researched book contains information for both novice and advanced turkey hunters on every facet of turkey hunting. **$15.50 each**

Name_____

Address _____

City _____State____ Zip_____

Send check or money order to:
Night Hawk Publications, P.O. Drawer 375, Fairfield, AL 35064
Ph (205)786-3630; 786-4022
For Visa or Master Card orders call toll free 1-800-627-4295
Or fax credit card order to (205)781-0927
Please allow 4 weeks for delivery